MANAGED MISCHIEF

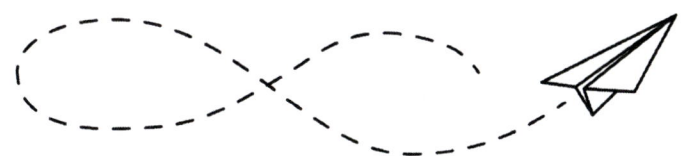

MANAGED MISCHIEF

A TOOLKIT OF IMPROV-INSPIRED GAMES

MANDY KHOSHNEVISAN

MANAGED MISCHIEF Copyright © 2016 by Mandana Khoshnevisan.

All rights reserved. Printed in the United States of America. No part of this book may be used or reproduced in any manner whatsoever without written permission except in the case of brief quotations embodied in critical articles or reviews.

For information:
Email: info@royapublications.com
Visit: www.royapublications.com

Cover design by Mandana Khoshnevisan

ISBN: 978-1-944218-06-5 (Trade Paperback)

ISBN: 978-1-944218-05-8 (e-book)

First Edition: December 2016

10 9 8 7 6 5 4 3 2 1

CONTENTS

A NOTE FROM THE AUTHOR	V
INTRODUCTION	IX
PART ONE: BACKGROUND	
1: USING THIS BOOK	21
PART TWO: MANAGING	
2: SKILLS FOR THE FACILITATOR	33
3: SEE WHAT'S HAPPENING; HELP IT HAPPEN	41
4: ON PLAYING GAMES	49
5: SKILLS FOR EVERYONE	63
6: A STARTER KIT	69

PART THREE: MISCHIEF

    7: GAMES FOR SEEING WHAT'S HAPPENING   79

    8: GAMES FOR HELPING IT HAPPEN   109

    9: MAKING OFFERS WITH YOUR VOICE   125

    10: GAMES FOR CIRCLES   133

    11: BALL GAMES   149

    12: MAKING OFFERS WITH YOUR PHYSICALITY   171

    13: SHARING CONTROL   221

    14: MAKING OFFERS WITH YOUR STORIES   243

EPILOGUE   265

APPENDIX THE FIRST: STATUS   269

APPENDIX THE SECOND: LISTS   297

BIBLIOGRAPHY   303

INDEX OF GAMES   305

TABS

Here's a delightfully analog way to navigate the games by thumbing through the book. At right are a series of icons that describe aspects of each game: if you're looking for a writing activity, for example, just thumb through the book and scan the edges for a mark that lines up with the Writing icon.

The descriptors are loosely arranged top to bottom from quiet/focused to active/loud.

Focus
Quiet Time
Writing
Art
Music
Memory
Verbal
Physical
Rapid-Fire
Partners
Circle
Group
Audience

 Focus

 Quiet Time

 Writing

 Art

 Music

 Memory

 Verbal

 Physical

 Rapid-Fire

 Partners

 Circle

 Group

 Audience

A NOTE FROM THE AUTHOR

The Section Before the Book Where I Talk About Myself
Or: Who am I anyway?

Greetings! Nice to meet you, dear reader. Take a second and pat yourself on the back for me, for taking the chance on this book. Who am I, you ask? At the time of writing, I've been studying and performing improvisational theater for almost 20 years, so I can call myself a professional improvisor. Most of my gainful employment as an adult has involved working with children, theater, and improv, so I'm also therefore a professional arts educator. These two vocations have given me the experience and excitement to write this book — though both of them would be a surprise to my younger self.

Yet, I've actually been working with kids and theater since about age 11. This twist of fate happened at the Youth Cultural Program, a really great four-week summer day camp run by the local branch of the AAUW.[1] At the ripe old age of 11, I was too old to be a camper anymore, but I wanted to volunteer so that I could keep going there. As a very shy kid, I had my heart set on helping the art teacher, in her nice, quiet classroom — but the art teacher already had enough help, so instead I was assigned to the new drama and folklore teacher. Such is fate. Right

---

1   American Association of University Women. A large part of their mission is to promote educational opportunities for girls and women (though this camp was co-ed).

away, I started helping her teach theater exercises, and she put me in charge of telling the folklore stories to the campers. She decided I should be the one to tell the stories, and so I believed her; I was just following directions. Suddenly I, a really shy kid, was now somehow in charge of speaking to the whole class on a regular basis. I grew to love this role: I would read the stories ahead of time, and then tell them to the children, without book or notes. This, though I didn't know it, was my first improv training: figuring out the important parts of the story, and improvising the steps between them.

    I volunteered at that camp all the way through high school, and slowly started getting more interested and more involved in performing theater myself. I did one musical my junior year of high school, then joined the drama class for the last half of my senior year. I loved performing, but there was a lot of stage fright there, too; performing always meant sweaty palms, pounding heart, and nausea.

    Then, during my freshman year of college, I started doing improv[2] — which, without my realizing it, erased my stage fright so completely that the revelation itself was startling and alarming to me. Near the end of freshman year, I was playing Rosie in our dorm dining hall production of *Bye Bye, Birdie*. Standing backstage before the first performance, waiting to go on within minutes, I realized that we'd only had one dress rehearsal and this would be the first time doing the whole show with the whole orchestra there at once, in front of all our friends… why on earth wasn't I scared to death? In fact, it hadn't even occurred to me to be scared! What a terrifying new feeling! But I'd learned from improv that … everything was going to be okay.

---

[2]   I went with a friend from my dorm, who had done improv in high school. She lasted about four or five rehearsals, then dropped out because of other interests. Me? I was hooked.

MANAGED MISCHIEF — AUTHOR'S NOTE

Who hath wrought this miracle? Patricia Ryan Madson started the improvised theater program at Stanford, having herself worked with Keith Johnstone (creator of TheatreSports and one of the world's capital-letter Improv Gurus). She taught acting at Stanford for several years before introducing improv to the drama department. She started the Stanford Improvisors in 1991 so that she could continue to coach advanced students who were interested in continuing to study and perform. I started my college improv journey in the safety of a more casual spinoff group, and then I studied with Patricia for the next four years. The overarching major lesson that I learned from my first taste of improv was: I could leap into the unknown without fear of falling. That's what made the stage fright disappear. Unlike a certain cartoon coyote, I learned to stride out over thin air, confident that even if I looked down, I would make it to the other side no matter what.

Because Patricia's classes at Stanford are for actual course credit, they were fun, but also very mindful, analytical, and theory-based. We learned to be students, actors, playwrights, storytellers, teachers, and critics, all at the same time. Patricia also practices and teaches Constructive Living,[3] so she always made sure to draw clear connections in class between improvising onstage and "improvising" in real life.[4] I learned a lot of things in college, but studying improv with Patricia helped me learn how to manage being a person. Now, as a grown-up,[5] I find myself making my living at all the things that I pined for as a child: I take turns being a teacher, a dancer, a puppeteer, a voiceover artist, a musician, an actor...

---

3   Constructive Living is based on two Japanese psychotherapies; certified instructors teach people to approach life realistically and thoughtfully. Its two aspects emphasize recognizing situations and being present, helpful, and purposeful; and appreciating the present and past for what they are.
4   For more about this kind of mindful living with improv principles, check out her book *Improv Wisdom*!
5   Sort of.

and I teach other people how to improvise. As someone who's benefited greatly from the life effects of the art form, and also as a teacher myself, every year of teaching I become more convinced of how great it would be if kids (and their caretakers) could benefit from the principles behind improvisation. Which brings me to … why this book?

INTRODUCTION

The Section of this Book that Functions Like an Introduction Except I Wrote it Myself

Why this book?

I wanted to write this book based on my own experiences learning and teaching improv. There are already a lot of great books out there about the subject.[1] Most of these books are directed either at drama teachers or seasoned improvisors, with the goal of training students to be better onstage performers. I thought, why not invite more people to play these improv games, with the goal of training students to be better at being themselves? Some people want to be performers, and some don't, but everyone can benefit from learning to be more comfortable in their own creativity and their interactions with others. I also want to help people who may NOT be too familiar with theater, but who are parents, teachers, and other child-associated adults, and who may be looking for fun games that might also secretly be educational. (Or heck, play these games with your adult-type friends; I certainly do!) The games and exercises and fun-things-to-do in this book are selected to provide a group experience that doesn't require a separate audience, and to meanwhile sneakily train the players to be inclusive, constructive, and fun to play with.

---

1   Check the bibliography for a list!

This book is also about having fun together in a low-pressure environment. When you're learning improv for performance, there are a lot of things to keep track of: Cheat out! Be louder! Remember where you put the imaginary door! Work on your accents! As a result, the various things you need to remember just keep piling up. As an actor and a professional improvisor, I DO think all those details are very important; I want performed improv to be meaningful theater, and theater requires rehearsal. But the basic principles of the art form can be boiled down to some very simple ideas, which practicing on their own in everyday life can yield delightful rewards. The games in this book, while being fun and weird and silly, were not curated into this collection in order to teach presentational drama skills, directly; instead, they help develop human interaction skills. Players can learn a lot that these games have to teach, without worrying about playing to a separate audience.

Another goal of mine in putting together a collection of games that aren't specifically performance-oriented is to prioritize ideas of growth and cooperation separately from the idea of "talent." In a regular improv book or another children's drama book geared towards getting kids onstage, it's possible to pick and choose the games that are likely to showcase skills that some people are already good at. Often, if playing a performative game in an informal (or even formal) setting generates a lot of audience laughter, the result is not to examine it any further than just celebrating the kids who are already funny and performative, thereby accidentally alienating the kids that might have a lot of room to grow.

My focus is to build ensemble, to be inclusive, to celebrate and bring together all the ways to think and solve problems and be clever and successful, not just the ones that immediately stick out as being "funny," especially since unhelpful behavior often makes an audience laugh. (Though people think of improv as comedy-based, one of the first things a good improv teacher will tell you is, Don't try to be funny.) We want the shy kids and the loudmouths and the revolutionaries and the teacher's pets to all come together, appreciate each other, and learn from each other's behavior.

I've also observed, and it's been corroborated by studies,[2] that kids are having a hard time on the playground ... finding things to do. About fifteen years ago, I was working in a day care (in a pretty well-to-do area). We had substantial periods of outside playtime each day, and so we spent a total of at least two hours a day in the lovely large playground, full of trees, play structures, paths, sandboxes, and grass. My task was to observe the children and help them if they needed me. Now, I remember that when I was a kid we would have epic games of pretend that would last for weeks or months. We chose characters, developed backstories for those characters, and created whole pretend worlds mapped out onto the existing environment; we would spend forever just making pretend food with leaves. We had a great time. Many of these sad three- and four-year-olds, the ones who weren't riding bikes or climbing on things, were just kind of absently wandering around. They didn't know what to do with themselves. I remember that only a few could even sustain a few minutes of pretend, let alone weeks of a continuing storyline. And this was fifteen years ago! I'm seeing kids today having an even harder time pretending. They're kids! Pretending is practically their job!

Researchers have been examining the shrinking of our attention spans: is it TV?[3] Social media? Screen time? Overscheduling? Sedentary lifestyle? Whatever it is, my fellow theater teachers also claim that kids are

---

2   Kyung Hee Kim published a study in 2011 called "The Creativity Crisis," wherein she examines people's scores on the Torrance Creativity Test from the 1960s through the 2000s. Kim finds that, though IQ scores in the US are going up, creativity scores are going down—especially since 1990, and especially among children in grades K-6. A *Newsweek* article called "The Creativity Crisis" (7/10/10) compares Kim's study and a few others about creativity, and investigates the impact on adult creativity and success.

3   The University of Washington provides a huge list of links to studies of TV and how it affects health and behavior: http://depts.washington.edu/tvhealth/studies.htm

having a harder time paying attention in class, so at least the anecdotal evidence is not mine alone.

Children's occupation and vocation is to play, and in order to play, you have to pay attention. Playing involves investigating your environment and coming up with ways to interact with it. Playing is the scientific method. Whether our inner desire and ability to play has been leached out of us by screen time and instantly-available information, or whether it's been trained out of us by adult life, we could all use a little reminder of the simple joys of exploring the people and things around us. While we're playing these games, we're secretly practicing how to pay attention and be present in the world. Play, meditation, science, art… they're all about learning to be an observer of the present, and about learning to trust yourself and your ideas about what's inside, and outside, your head.

Improv is something you can do together with the kids in your life, and it's also something you can teach them to do on their own, so that they're not afraid of time with "nothing" to do. It's a very useful skill, finding a game using your environment and your imagination. Building something from nothing, using just the things and people around you, requires some basic cooperation skills as well. By teaching kids to think like improvisors, we're helping them be fun to play with, now and hopefully in the future.

Improv skills can also translate from playtime to regular-life-time. The skills of observation, deduction and even empathy, developed by playing creative and cooperative games, come in pretty handy in most situations. For example, they're useful for helping children examine and understand things that are going wrong in their environment. Even if the problem can't be fixed directly, if someone can merely name and identify the problem (pointing out that they see what's happening), everyone can feel like they've got just a bit more control and agency over an unfortunate situation. If you're in charge of a group of children and something's happening that's not ideal and no one can really do anything about it, merely publicly *acknowledging* and affirming the observation that something is wrong can help children be more confident in their *own* perceptions, and thus be able to tough it out. For example, if it's hot in the room but the heat is controlled centrally and you can't turn it off, just saying, "Boy, guys, it's really hot in here, isn't it?" is usually enough to stop the brunt of the complaints. Because you've consciously pointed out that you also notice the obvious situation and are affected by it, your small charges can see that all of you are in the same boat.

The same principle not only applies to the physical state of the room, but to the emotional state of the people in it. If there's something going on with you or the situation that's making it harder for you to deal with your charges — you have a headache, or you're feeling mad or sad — it's better to explain that than to try to pretend nothing's wrong. Small people are extremely perceptive, and if something's wrong, they can tell. It's better for you to tell them the truth, rather than let them draw conclusions that may be damaging, such as "you hate me," or "you're mad at me" — or, "you lie to us." This, along with modeling empathy for the kids when they have the same issues, can make things easier on you. You don't need to "put up a front" — or, essentially, lie — in order to keep control of things ... all the kids will learn from that is that you're untrustworthy.

If you separate these skills from the stage, and bring them directly into your daily life and practical interactions, then it means you can practice being delightful and creative and constructive all the time, in all sorts of pursuits. Writing, dancing, making music, making art, problem-solving ... all these and more require the kinds of thinking that improv can help you with. By working on these skills, you learn to accept yourself as a creative person, and then you're unstoppable.

My hope for this book is that those who read it and try things out will end up spreading these improv principles to everyone they know, and soon everyone all over the world will be friendly and creative all the time, and there'll be world peace! (Well, one can always dream.)

My slightly more down-to-earth hope is that playing these games will foster a fun, creative and mutually respectful ensemble in your environment, whether it be a classroom, a camp, a living room, or just the occasional car ride. These are games you can play in a structured environment as part of a larger curriculum, or in an unstructured environment when you might need something fun to keep you and your charges occupied.

A side effect of reading this book might be that by playing these games with children, educators and parents might absorb some of the accompanying principles into their own daily lives, and use them to have more fun with that crazy and unpredictable task that is being in charge of children. These games are fun to play, and if you're going to really use them in class, there's some philosophy behind this improv thing that you might want to give a go.

Drama teachers are trained to do this whole performance thing, but teaching and parenting are actually also forms of performance, and I think many teachers and other people who are put in charge of small people don't get a lot of practical training with actually DEALING with those small people, who (surprise) turn out to be just as individual and idiosyncratic as you and me. For some, relating to these small strangers is easier than for others, and if it feels scary for you, you might feel the need to put on a personality that's not your own. You might feel the need to "pretend" to be an authority figure, using traits you think authority figures should have, or using techniques you remember from the authority figures of your youth. It's important to set limits and so forth, to have a safe and comforting environment for everyone, but I think people get intimidated by the notion that *they're* the one in charge ... it's completely normal to feel like something of a fraud at the realization that the man behind the curtain is ... you.

Two common shortcuts to feeling in control are: 1, Saying no to things, and 2, Issuing (possibly arbitrary) commands and/or punishments. The problem there is that generally children are great at seeing the truth. And if they can see that, out of insecurity, you're acting against your own instincts or the obvious logical thing to do ("It's hot in here, can we open the window?" "*No.*" "Why not?" "Because I said so.") then they start to believe that they can't trust you. Then it becomes a downward spiral: You have to assert your grip tighter, and they start to squirm away even harder. There are studies that prove that people will accept a judgment against them, as long as they agree that the rules are fair.[4] The assertion of arbitrary authority, on the other hand, merely for the sake of enforcing authority, causes resentment and mistrust. Kids who are treated as if they are bad because they don't "obey" start to embrace the role of the bad kid simply because that's the only role left for them.

One thing I've noticed while teaching in schools during the school day, getting to observe their regular teachers and environments, was the way in which those environments affected the kids. I could see that the teacher's personality had a huge impact on the class's personality and overall dynamic. At one school I worked at, there were three different classes participating in the theater program. The goals of the program were to have each class put on a short play involving all the students; each class performed a different international folktale. The first class in the schedule had a new teacher who seemed inexperienced and somewhat

---

4   In the *Harvard Business Review*, January 2003, there's an article called "Fair Process: Managing in the Knowledge Economy", and it cites a study that concluded, "In this article, W. Chan Kim and Renée Mauborgne describe one such process, which grew out of their research into the links between trust, idea sharing, and corporate performance. Their central finding is that employees will commit to a manager's decision—even one they disagree with—if they believe that the process the manager used to make the decision was fair."

harried. She tended to raise her voice a lot and threaten punishments, correcting behavior that wasn't necessarily disruptive but that she just happened not to like for some reason. Plus, she didn't always seem to follow up on her pronouncements, which means those punishments were mostly empty threats.[5] Her class tended to be shy and reticent to act in front of each other (they got there eventually), but also sassy, critical of each other, and hard to calm down and wrangle.

The second teacher was more experienced, and her class pretty average in their attentiveness and participation.

The third teacher projected an aura of serenity. She led her class in periodic stretching breaks, standing and bending and twisting. They got to pick which songs to listen to while working, and which educational videos to watch in the small stretches of waiting time between activities. They were a delight for me to work with.

The most amazing classroom I ever experienced as an outreach teacher was a sixth grade classroom in a public school near San Jose, California, in an area that has a high population of low-income families. That teacher (who used to be a monk, by the way) had built his own little world inside that classroom. He'd made the whole class into an immersive Harry Potter wonderland: the class sat in four different "houses" around the room, and individuals or groups could win points for their houses, just like in the books. They were also physically active: they played Quiddich on the playground, at recess and sometimes as part of class. He'd built a working kitchen from scratch in the back of the classroom, and the kids routinely cooked food. When I and my teaching partner showed up

---

5   "If you don't stop _____, I'm going to _____." was a common phrase I heard. The trouble with that kind of thing is that the activity and the consequence are often both vague, and the issuer of the edict probably doesn't actually want to carry out the consequence because it would be annoying and inconvenient to both parties. The upshot is that neither involved party changes their behavior, and now everyone's also annoyed and grouchy.

on the first day, he offered us leftover eggplant parmesan, and wouldn't let us put the dishes in the sink: "The kids'll take care of it." He had a system for kids who couldn't focus: there were a couple of isolation stations in the room, desks facing the wall and corralled off with poster board, where kids could put themselves when they needed to cool off and remove themselves from distractions. He could be very stern and his rules were firm, but no one was scared of him; they adored him. His students were amazing and helpful to us as well. Our assignment was to help each sixth-grade class in the school write and perform their own Greek myth play, and his students wrote one with a song in it. It was their idea. His students practiced on their own on days we weren't there; they made up their own choreography and blocking. They were not embarrassed to sing and dance, to try new things, or to offer us their artistic work. They raised the expectations of the other students in the other classes. By being a great example, that class motivated everyone's achievements.

What these exciting teachers have in common is that they didn't make it a secret that they "saw" their students. They said yes to the children's needs, basic needs that people often try to pretend don't exist, or pretend that they themselves don't have. It can be easy to forget that children are also human beings. Sometimes teachers expect things of students that they would never expect of, say, other adults — like, for example, sitting still for hours without even fidgeting. Children need to get up and stretch. Children need to run around. Children need to learn with their bodies. The stretching teacher gave them breaks in order to help them clear their minds and get in touch with their kinesthetic awareness.[6] Children need to play games. Children need to deal with information in different ways. Children need to learn to work together happily. Children need to learn to explore all their talents. Cooking is measuring, following directions,

---

6   I am *amazed* by the number of children I encounter in elementary school drama classes who are so inflexible that they can't even touch their toes.

improvising, using real-world skills. Playing a sport is remembering rules, counting points, making strategies, exercising judgment, working together. Children have interests that are real. The Quiddich teacher used the Harry Potter universe because it's something kids really like and know a lot about. Instead of labeling their interests as distractions that should be separated from the classroom, he embraced them, and *over*-accepted them, making that structure an integral part of his teaching structure for the entire year. Children need to know that you, the educator/facilitator, will listen to them, tell them the truth, and be fair. Improv principles at work!

PART ONE:

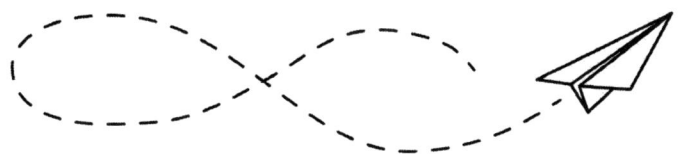

BACKGROUND

USING THIS BOOK

Who This Book is For and How to Use It

Who are these games for?

The short answer is: they're for everyone. There are *lots* of improv games out there. I compiled this list based on games that I use in my teaching because they work well with children in the K-12 grades, because they teach the concepts that I think are the most useful and constructive, and because I like them and I think they're fun (which is important). When I tried, then, to go through and sort them into age groups, I just kept categorizing all the games as being for "everyone." There are a very few that work better if the players are pretty fluent with the concepts of writing and spelling, so they probably wouldn't be generally appropriate for ages three through six, though there are certainly exceptions.

But, I fully stand by the assertion that even if games have a lower age limit, they absolutely do not have an upper age limit. Everyone, everyone, everyone can play these games together. Players of different ages and competencies can get different benefits from them, and can discover different things about them. But even if a game feels like it's for "babies," that's even more reason for adults to play it!

How do I use this book?

The information in this book comes from my 20 years of training in improvisation, and my lots-of-years using theater and improv skills in a wide variety of contexts, from directing fully staged musicals to teaching preschool to babysitting. I learned a great many games from a wide variety of great teachers and books, some of which are here as I learned them, and some of which I've modified over the years — only a couple of the games in here are ones I've made up. All of these games are ones that I've had a lot of fun playing in these varied contexts, and they're ones that children also enjoy.

So now that you're reading this book at this very moment, you can use it any way you wish. The beginning section about improv philosophy is one that I recommend everyone read, if you're planning to play any of these games. It's helpful to have some pertinent background before proceeding. Even if you're not planning on directly explaining it to the game-players you have in mind, you as a facilitator should still play the games with your own eye on the underlying principles.

After soaking up some philosophy, you can dive into the game section looking for treasures. I've arranged the chapters by presenting the concepts in the order in which I'd normally introduce them to a group of students.

The first three skills, the Super Basics of "Seeing What's Happening," are games I play on the first day with almost everyone of any age who's learning about improv (whether we're consciously learning about it through structured lessons, or secretly soaking up the skills while we work on something else, like rehearsing a play).

After the Super Basics, the categories of games are arranged in roughly the order in which I usually do them on any given day, the way I typically arrange a class:

- I start by picking three activities that warm up the group in three different ways: connecting to each other, warming up bodies, and moving through space to explore our environment. (Often I work in that order, although your methods may vary: some groups need an energy release before coming together in a circle, for example.) Usually I try to choose warmups that will tap into skills they'll be drawing on later in the day's main lesson — but that's not necessary.
- **Connecting and centering:** We'll start in a circle, and usually play a word-at-a-time game or another circle game that requires focus (see the Circle Games, page 133).
- **Warming up muscles and movement:** Next we might play a ball game or other physicality game, still in a circle (such as Fill the Space, page 179 or I am a Tree, page 187)
- **Moving through space:** Next we might break out of the circle into the room and do some other physical activities like Spacewalk, Find the Thing, Imaginary Activity, etc. (See the chapter on Physicality, page 171).
- **Main Idea:** When I'm teaching a class that's specifically improv, the day's main focus often falls under the umbrella of one of the chapters in this book, and I'll move on to play one or several games from that chapter (physicality, storytelling, status, etc.). Even if your class isn't an improv class — creative writing, art, history, science, P.E., dance, who knows? — you can still prepare your students for the rest of your lesson using the games in this book.

Within each chapter, the games are arranged roughly in order of complexity, so that each game tends to build on the skills of the previous games. If I were going to play multiple games in a single category (either on the same day, or in sequence throughout a curriculum), I'd play them in the order in which they appear here.

You can also, of course, play any of the games in the book at any time, whenever you feel like it. The games often fit into many categories at once, and can be easily adapted or tweaked as you see fit: maybe a particular game or its variation would help illustrate a history lesson in your classroom, or another would help everyone in your camp remember each other's names, or another would entertain kids in an organized way at a birthday party or a day in the park. You can present these games as alternatives to screen time, or play them in the car, or while waiting at a restaurant or airport. These games would also be good for warming up cooperation skills before doing an unrelated group activity (like working on a small-group project in a classroom, for example). And they would be great as part of a more organized, specifically-structured improv time. Kids can even learn to play these games all on their own. (Or, you can play them with your adult friends with no children present! I do.) It's up to you how you want to use them! Try them out! You're not going to break them.

For each game, there's a sequence of icons telling you what kind of game it is: multiple games and their variations can work different improv "muscles" or be more effective in certain circumstances. Then, in the back of the book, there are lists of games for various circumstances: in the car, outside in the yard or the park, games for two, games with creative writing, games with music, games with drawing, games with big physicality and games for quiet time. Plus, you can feel free to adapt these games to fit your own purpose. See what happens if you have an idea for a different way to play them or a different context in which to use them!

Children often have ideas of other ways to play games. It's fun to notice when that's happening, and follow it where it's leading you. An idea for a variation might end up not working well, but there's no reason not to at least give it a try. It's usually worth following players' ideas about how to play a game differently. Why not? You might stumble onto something amazing that you don't want to stop exploring.

For example, what if you told a story, maybe one word at a time, set in an imaginary country? At the end of the story, maybe you're fascinated by that country you created, and want to find out more about it. Maybe you could draw a map of it together, each adding one thing at a time. Then maybe you could draw pictures of some people who live there, each adding one thing at a time … Maybe you could pretend to be those characters, and act out your story, or a new story, or maybe you could write letters from those characters to each other, one word at a time … It could become a game that goes on and on through days or weeks of revisiting that world and those characters. One idea could unlock a massive cascade of creativity.

How can I teach these games if I've never played them before?

Short answer: read the directions and try them out together!

Improv teaches you a lot of life skills, secretly, that they just don't teach in school. Until now! *You* can teach them! I hereby formally deputize you. Whether you're a shy person or an outgoing person, whether you think of yourself as an "artistic type" or not, *you* can lead these games and teach them to children — *if* you in turn agree to have fun trying it out. You can all learn together.

These games and exercises are for teachers/facilitators/parents who may say, "But I'm not an actor!" As I often tell people (usually skeptical people at parties and whatnot), if you can have a conversation, you're improvising. I hope to take the scariness of "acting" out of the mix. Artistic pursuits tend to scare the bejinkies out of people, and then they get paranoid and pass on their fear to others. People — especially adults, but starting around age seven or eight — think to themselves, Oh, but I can't sing ... I can't draw ... I can't act ... I can't dance. You *can*. YOU CAN. Do it, and you're doing it. Learning improv had a much larger impact on me than I was expecting. I *thought* it would be fun and challenging. I *discovered* that it erased my stage fright, and made me a lot less shy in public. Heck, standing in front of large groups of strangers is my job now!

Learning and teaching improv with a group of kids may very well similarly allow you to get in touch with your own productive creativity. You don't have to wait for the mythical hand of Something to reach down and hand you the Secret of Inspiration And Genius. The scary secret is, there is no secret. Just start trying to do something, and suddenly you're doing it. You can always learn to do something better by practicing, but the fundamentals exist within you already. The spirit of improv can help you do pretty much anything. The secret is, you don't *already* have to know what you're doing, in order to write or paint or make music or act or talk to people. Pretty much no one knows what they're doing, most of the time. Any of these creative or social activities you always wish you could do? *You can already do them!* You have everything it takes, already, to give them a try. And once you start practicing something, you can learn to do it better, and have fun doing it.

The daunting part of trying something new is that we don't already know everything about it, and we're afraid to look stupid by trying and failing. We want to be experts at everything right away. But guess what? It takes no experience to be a beginner.

(This applies to basically anything: "I can't do math! I can't program a computer! I can't run! I can't play basketball! I can't speak in front of people." Sure you can. Just give it a try, and then you've done it. Want to do it a little better? Try again!)

(This reluctance applies doubly to girls… I think girls tend to think that they must be missing something, that they can't possibly know as much as other people do, especially about science and math.[1] It's all a matter of confidence: Girls often do better in science and math, but boys tend to learn to pretend that they always know what they're doing, which intimidates girls, I think, and as school years pass, girls fall to the wayside feeling like they must not be gifted enough to be an expert.)

You don't need to be an expert to teach something; you just need to be curious and willing to find things out.[2] You can read through the instructions for one of these games, gather your group of charges, and

---

1   For example, AAUW has published several studies about gender equity in schools, including a 2010 study entitled "Why So Few? Women in Science, Technology, Engineering, and Mathematics." This study states the problem nicely: "The issue of self-assessment, or how we view our own abilities, is another area where cultural factors have been found to limit girls' interest in mathematics and mathematically challenging careers. Research profiled in the report finds that girls assess their mathematical abilities lower than do boys with similar mathematical achievements. At the same time, girls hold themselves to a higher standard than boys do in subjects like math, believing that they have to be exceptional to succeed in 'male' fields." ("Why So Few?" AAUW Executive Summary, p. 2)

2   One of my favorite high school English teachers, Mr. Ellis, let us vote on the books we were reading for AP English. There was an Approved List for the AP test, and at the end of every book we got to vote on the next book to read from the list. We chose *Brave New World*, and Mr. Ellis had never read it! I don't think I'd ever seen a teacher so delightedly gleeful about a class assignment; every day he was dying to talk to us about the latest chapters. He was discovering it just as we were, and he was extremely excited about it. He could have, I suppose, pretended he *had* read it; he was the teacher, after all, and one step ahead of us. But his glee was infectious, and it was amazing to us that he was so candidly excited and surprised by the book.

try it out. As a bonus, figuring out how to teach something to others helps you learn it, and by being conscious enough of the improv thought process to work through it with kids, teaching these games may bring to the forefront of your mind how to work this stuff into your daily life.

Sure, these games I write about are meant to be fun. But they're also meant to challenge some deeply ingrained habits, and therefore to reap the most benefit is going to take a tiny bit of concerted effort. In order to truly learn from the games, you've got to learn some things about yourself, and sometimes that's difficult. For this reason, it's most "educational" if someone in the group is keeping an eye on the fundamentals ... and that means that the person in charge is also going to have to keep an eye on themselves. I did say, everyone learns from each other, and everyone learns from themselves. That includes the teacher/parent/facilitator in the situation. The other players will learn from you, so it's best to make sure you're learning from yourself as well. That's why, before the section describing games, there's a whole part about that improv theory and philosophy stuff. If you're going to give these games a shot, you'll have the best results if you at least skim that part of the book. Really.

It might be a challenge. But you can do it!

On Ownership of These Games

Because improv is in some ways an oral tradition, with games and exercises passed around the world and modified, it is very difficult to determine exactly where many of these games actually originated. This book is primarily a compilation: most of these games I have learned over the years from excellent teachers and directors, some of whom learned them from other sources, and so on. Some I present with my own modifications developed over many years of teaching children; a select few I have made up (although who knows who else has independently also made up a similar game somewhere in the world?).

In general, for the aggregate of my improv knowledge and training, and a great deal of wisdom absorbed through osmosis, I am indebted to: Patrica Ryan Madson from Stanford University; many great coaches who were at BATS Improv in San Francisco including Rebecca Stockley, Paul Killam, Barbara Scott, J. Raoul Brody, Diane Rachel, William Hall, Regina Saisi, Tim Orr, Laura Derry, Rafe Chase, and Stephen Kearin; Dan O'Connor of Impro Theatre in L.A.; and my colleagues from the Un-Scripted Theater Company, including Christian Utzman, Tara McDonough, Dave Dyson, Alan Goy, and Susan Snyder. I am also indebted to Keith Johnstone, whose books I have learned much from, whose games and work I refer to in this book, and whose personal intelligence and humor I have appreciated immensely.

In specific, throughout the book, I try to cite sources for games when I can; I don't claim to have created any of them unless I specifically say so, and even then, it's only as far as I know.

You're welcome to continue the tradition, too ... read, modify, and make up a few games of your own.

PART TWO:

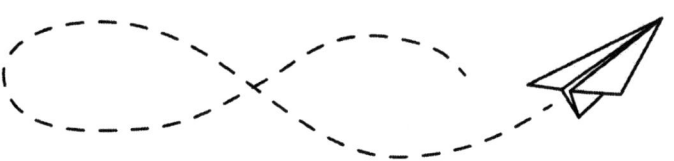

MANAGING

SKILLS FOR THE FACILITATOR

The Section of This Book That's About Preparing to Play Games

What's this Improv Thing, Anyway? Theory And Philosophy and Secret Information and Stuff

Improvisation is a pretty hot concept right now — specifically as it applies to offstage life.[1] The group based in New York that stages guerilla theatrical events in public spaces is even called Improv Everywhere, indicating that improvisation is transcending the stage. Articles are popping up all over the place in business-oriented publications like *Forbes*,[2] and *Bloomberg BusinessWeek*.[3] Theater companies around the world now routinely offer improv workshops as teambuilding and creativity consulting to all kinds of businesses. The Applied Improv Network is an international organization of professionals dedicated to sharing

---

1   Virtually every day I see new articles and videos circulating online about the power of improv in the real world—like Alan Alda's work with scientists and communication: "Attention, All Scientists: Do Improv, With Alan Alda's Help," *New York Times* (3/2/2015).
2   "Why Improv Training is Great for Business," Forbes.com (6/27/2014); "Can Improv Improve Marketing?" Forbes.com (12/1/2014) and the fantastically-titled "Groupon Proves Value of Brand Improv with Hilarious Handling of Banana Bunker," Forbes.com (3/31/2015) — just to select three random articles.
3   "How to Run Your Company Like an Improv Group, by Twitter CEO Dick Costolo" *Bloomberg.com* (4/11/2013).

the principles of improv with businesses and other organizations.[4] At Stanford, where I started studying the art form, Drama 103 (Intro to Improvisation) used to be required for the Mechanical Engineering graduate degree, and now the improv teachers there are collaborating with the designers at the Stanford Design School. My friend Rebecca Stockley is the resident improv teacher at Disney/Pixar, teaching storytelling for the writers and animators. As the art form gains more visibility in the world at large, and people are starting to find out that there's more to it than *Whose Line Is It, Anyway?*, improv is being more recognized as a set of concepts that might be valuable for regular people in everyday life, not just for playing games on a stage in order to make people laugh.

Wait — What's improv, you ask? What a good question! In my experience, when I say I do improv, most people reply, "Oh — like *Whose Line is it, Anyway?*" The other touchstone people have is in the context of forgetting lines. "Oh — like ad libbing?" When extracted from the dueling concepts of "only for goofy stage amusement," and "only when you're in trouble," what *does* it mean?

Here's what Merriam-Webster has to say about it:[5]

im•pro•vise

1: *to compose, recite, play, or sing extemporaneously*

2: *to make, invent, or arrange offhand*

3: *to make or fabricate out of what is conveniently on hand* <*improvise a meal*>

I love the combination of these three definitions, and I feel that it goes right to the heart of this book. Notice how the three definitions place all kinds of creation side by side, including not only speaking but also singing, inventing, building, and even *cooking*? Look at all those great verbs in there. That's exactly what I'm hoping: that these fun things to do

---

4   Find out more about them at: http://appliedimprov.ning.com

5   This is the online definition from merriam-webster.com.

that I set out will impart to you and yours the spirit of, "Yeah; I can do that!" No matter what the medium is, you can do it, and you can make a game of it.

So if "Improvisation-with-a-capital-I" isn't just for the stage and screen, what is it? The basic skills which allow you to play games together onstage also make it easier for you to: pay attention and listen to others, value your own ideas, accept others' ideas, read human behavior, allow yourself to share control, be constructive, and work together to make something happen. Improv is about playing well with others, honoring everyone's ideas to make a surprising and delightful thing together. That thing might be an improvised story or piece of music — or it might be a mural, a computer program, or a plan for a building. Those finely-tuned cooperation skills can help us equally in onstage and offstage situations.

How does this benefit our offstage life? Let's break it down:

Paying attention and listening

Especially in our strangely partisan culture, this might be hard to understand, but: paying attention to someone isn't equivalent to agreeing with them. (As Aristotle may have said, "It is the mark of an educated mind to be able to entertain a thought without accepting it.") Your mind is strong: you can listen to a statement or opinion you don't agree with, and still manage to maintain your own feelings and opinions. An idea you don't agree with can't hurt you.

During a conversation, whatever the other person has said is going to be important later, whether you're in an "improv scene," a classroom or a business meeting. Taking the time while they talk to plan your own response means you're not actually listening to what they're saying, and so when the time comes for you to respond, your response is actually going to have little to do with their statement. But pay attention with all your focus, and you'll understand better what they have to say. This might make it easier for you to interact with people you don't "like" or agree with. When you've paid attention, you don't have to agree with them; you just have to "hear" them. Kat Koppett, author of *Training to Imagine*, said once in a workshop that when companies are requesting some teambuilding help and they tell you what they want, they most approve of your strategy if you communicate it to them using the very words they used. They want you to mirror themselves back to themselves. The company, just like a conversation partner, wants first and foremost to know they've been heard.[6]

Valuing your own ideas

Improv teaches you that you don't need to ignore your own ideas for being "weird" or "not good enough"; you can present them with confidence. When you start learning to improvise, you learn pretty quickly that everyone's spontaneous ideas seem pretty darn weird. You also learn that when you let yourself express some of your ideas, there will be other ideas close behind. Letting them flow out means that the other ideas following close behind can also flow out, fast on their heels. Sometimes you'll notice, in a scene or a brainstorming session, that you've created a mental and verbal logjam: you've thought of an idea, but it's so "bad" that you can't possibly bring yourself to say it, and now you can't think of anything else. If you let doubt dam up your river of ideas, you'll

---

6   *Training to Imagine* is a great resource and toolkit for improv activities that promote teamwork, creativity, and leadership specifically in a business environment. If the exercises in this book seem like fun and you're looking for more complicated games to play with adults, check out Kat's book!

never be able to let yourself think of anything. If, on the other hand, you give yourself permission to quickly generate a lot of ideas, it feels safer to triage them later. If you have to solve a problem, and you list all the possible solutions you can think of, then of course some will be more viable than others. It's OK to point out that some of your own ideas — gasp! — probably won't work. But if you generate enough ideas, some of them are bound to be great, and one of those may indeed be the right solution to your specific problem.

It's like photography: the way to get a really great photo is to take a heck of a lot of photos and sort through them later. One of them is going to be really great. No one needs to see the others. Yet, because we don't see all the photos that were taken, we think that the one brilliant photo was the only one, and it was just perfect the first time. Nope! The secret to the creative process is that often there is no secret, and you just keep trying things until you stumble into something brilliant.

Valuing others' ideas and sharing control

Because through practicing improv you learn to be confident that you'll always be able to think of something when you need to, you learn that you don't have to cling so tightly to an idea that just doesn't fit the current situation. If your idea's time has come and gone, you'll have another one soon. And championing someone else's idea instead of your own doesn't have to feel like a "defeat." On the contrary, it helps you be constructive: a lot of these exercises and games depend on agreeing to someone's input before you can move on with your own input. The result of such give-and-take is not "one person's idea," but something that everyone built together, all relying on each other. Valuing someone else's idea often means giving up the feeling of sole control, but the group result is usually something that no one person's mind could think of alone, and therefore that much more powerful.

Seeing the whole picture

Practicing improvisation also teaches you, through paying attention with multiple senses, that it's possible to not only listen carefully to what someone is saying, but to pick up on what someone is *not* saying. By allowing yourself to pay full attention to someone, observing even their tone of voice and body language, you can interpret more of, not just what they say, but what they *mean*. It can make you more conscious of other people's behavior, and of the effect your own behavior can have on someone else.

Being friends with failure

The concept of grit in education is gaining traction nowadays. Children who are taught that they should never fail are afraid that if they ever make a mistake at anything, they'll fall right out the bottom of life forever. Or else, they'll do poorly at something once, and figure because they're not good at it right away, that they should stop doing it because things are supposed to be easy. Having grit is defined as, basically, not giving up because the going is momentarily tough; if you have grit, you have resilience and determination. No matter what your natural ability may be, approaching life with a growth mindset makes you more likely to succeed at whatever it is you've put your mind to. Practicing improv can help you embrace, or at least move past, failures big and small. You learn that you can always pick yourself up again, or let someone help you up.

Mastering your built-in skills

As an added bonus, doing improv with children helps them exercise their facility and confidence in their natural and developing skills of voice, body, and mind. Playing these simple games can give them more practice with language, vocal projection, physical expressiveness, and miscellaneous motor skills. Keith Johnstone in his book *Impro* talks a lot about having been a physically restricted teenager, slumping and embarrassed, with a lisp, afraid to do anything with his mind or his body as a result of a rigid British education that encouraged ramrod-straight students:

> "... I began to see myself as *crippled in the use of myself* (just as a great violinist would play better on a cheap violin than I would on a Strad). My breathing was inhibited, my voice and posture were wrecked, something was seriously wrong with my imagination — it was becoming difficult actually to get ideas. [...] I'd left school with worse posture, and a worse voice, with worse movement and far less spontaneity than when I'd entered it."[7]

By merely playing these games for fun and exploration, and not putting pressure on the public performance aspect, the players are rehearsing their natural abilities; the more they develop their skills, the more successful the games will be for them, because they've improved their abilities to understand and be understood.

Improvising, especially playing these games, requires utilizing a lot of verbal skills: listening comprehension, verbal repetition, vocabulary building, and storytelling, to name a few. Not to mention, playing many

---

7   *Impro*, pp. 16-17.

of the games exercises merely the simple skill of speaking aloud, and loud enough for other people to hear you.

Moving improvisationally, without the pressure of performance, lets kids experiment with strange and fun ways to move their bodies, without worrying so much that they look "weird." It seems like a particularly Western problem to me, that of reduced physical activity and looseness. Westernized countries such as the United States and Britain don't have a lot of dance or traditional movement built into their national culture. We are people taught to sit still indoors, as children and as adults. As a result, lots of children grow up not knowing how to dance, or how to move. We don't know what to do with our bodies, in movement or at rest. Having mastery over our own movements can go a long way towards building self-confidence.

As a child who was both verbally and physically shy, both aspects of the work were invaluable to me once I started doing improv in college. Learning to explore my verbal and physical capabilities meant learning more about myself as a person. That in turn led to discovering how to present to the world a more authentic version of myself.

SEE WHAT'S HAPPENING; HELP IT HAPPEN

My Own Improv Mantra

Now that you've got some philosophy and personal testimony, how does one go about actually learning how to *do* this thing called improv? I'd say, start with the simple and obvious. "See what's happening; help it happen."

I developed this, my own improv mantra, out of necessity, while I was teaching high school students.[1] Teaching at Menlo School, in the San Francisco Bay Area, was a fun and challenging experience. I taught improv there a few times a year for about 10 years, working with and for the high school's full-time amazing drama teacher.[2] Menlo is a high-achieving school whose students are working and committing their time past capacity; everyone does everything. It's the only school I've worked at where the jocks *are* the drama stars, and have to choose between being in the musical and playing lacrosse, football, water polo, and/or baseball. These kids are *busy*. Because of how busy the students were, and because of how much other theater was also usually going on at the same time, my improv teaching challenges were always those of scarcity.

---

1   Necessity: the mother of this and of many other inventions.
2   Thanks, Beth!

It was exciting because with every session I had to re-evaluate what I was going to teach them, in order to fill the present challenge in the time allotted. One year, we did a show that was half shortform scenes and games, half narrative longform (pieces that were 20 to 40 minutes long, following a single storyline like a short movie or play). One year, we did a modified version of a format called "Storybox" (created by Chicago Improv Festival producer Jonathan Pitts), a format which mandates that the group work together with extreme efficiency and solid group mind to tell the story of one character. Every show was a new and different artistic challenge.

Every show was also challenging because of the amount and arrangement of the students' available rehearsal time. I kept starting the year off with less and less time in which to stage a show, until one year I had two weeks, and what boiled down to about seven rehearsals which not everyone could come to, in which to set up and stage two ninety-minute shows. Plus, at least half of my students had not performed with me before, and some had never done improv before, and a couple had never really done theater, either. That year, I sat myself down and thought, "What is the *bare minimum* that these kids need to know in order to improvise together?" At the time, I was also working with the Un-Scripted Theater Company in San Francisco. Doing the kind of longform, theatrical, genre-specific improv that we did, we found that we had to do a lot of "un-teaching" of the kind of skills that people often learn in beginning improvisation. Intermediate adult improvisors can overgeneralize the lessons they learn as beginners, so they often tend to be unrealistically postitive — *too* accepting, *too* ready to jump on the first bandwagon, *too* blindly and immediately agreeable at the expense of the more complex and more human storyline. How could I short-circuit that path, I wondered, and get my high school students right to the spot I need them to be, in order to be onstage confidently? And so I developed my two-clause mantra: "See what's happening; help it happen."

There's a lot packed in there, at multiple levels of interpretation. To "see" what's "happening," you have to be paying attention to surface details: who's there, where's the story taking place, etc. But there's also, inherent in the clause, the prod to look deeper, beyond just "hearing words"; you have to put two and two together, so to speak, to really *see* what's going on at more of a subtext level. Is the prince trying to oust his twin brother? Is the customer trying to get away without paying? Is the princess unhappy being a princess? Your job is always to get at the root of what's actually going on, the thing that a reader or an audience would recognize as the important part. What people are *saying* to each other is often the least important thing. The other thing about *seeing* is that it trains you to read cues such as body language, and to read meaning in the way people are using their bodies to display emotions, to portray characters, and to define the space they're in (by interacting with imaginary objects).

The next step, the "help it happen," bypasses a problem that the Un-Scripted Theater Company continuously had with trained improvisors — the "say yes" mantra. This, combined with a desire to keep things "positive," results in people acting strangely and unrealistically to create childlike stories that real children probably wouldn't enjoy very much. Adult improvisors in training often try too hard to do a "good job" at improv. As a result, they leap into their stories and try to pounce on the action, making the main conflict stem from an insignificant detail that a normal person actually in that situation would probably just ignore. By merely emphasizing "see what's happening, help it happen," you encourage players to use their own powers of logic, observation and judgment: they only need to scrutinize the story as it's occurred thus far, and participate in it however they seem to be needed in order to help the story happen.

If all they're thinking is, "See what's happening, help it happen," then they don't need to think too far into the future. They can just start from what they've seen so far, and do the thing that seems obvious. It's like the game Othello: a minute to learn, a lifetime to master. It's easy to begin, but once you go down the rabbit hole, there are lots of ways to make the nuances more nuanced. You can improve your theatrical performance, if you choose, by studying all the actor-y stuff: movement, voice, diction, dialects, etc. — but if you keep in mind that you just need to see what's happening and help it happen, everyone can play with everyone.

My two-week experiment turned out pretty darn great (if I do say so myself), considering the challenge posed.[3] And I realized while watching the rehearsals and especially the shows that those students did some things that seem "impossible" to experienced improvisors, because no one had ever told them that they were impossible. We had scenes with seventeen kids in them at once — scenes that actually made sense. I saw a scene unfold with a huge pack of kids onstage, evolving from a tableau, and it turned into a surreal little bit where everyone wound up wearing a chair on their head. Why? Because someone started it, and everyone else helped it happen. I was seeing things I'd never seen before, that were much more interesting than the usual "beginning improv" scenes I'd seen a million times. No one had given them a formula, so they weren't following one. Sometimes the conventional "establish Who, What, and Where in three sentences" can result in scenes that end up being artificially childish, because people are playing according to what they've been told are the rules. But when you have no rules except "notice

---

[3] My students even ran the show by themselves: I was sitting in the booth, occasionally advising the lighting improvisor and stage manager (also a student), but I didn't go onstage or otherwise interfere. They emceed, they introduced games, they asked for audience volunteers, they decided what games to play next … they did it all by themselves.

what rules have apparently evolved," you can create truly surprising and delightful stories.

The good improv teachers urge, "Play to the top of your intelligence!" Del Close, founder of The Committee, legendary director of Second City, and oft-cited improv guru, is known for saying, "Treat others as if they are poets, geniuses, and artists, and they will be."[4] If you allow yourself to really "see what's happening" according to your best, smartest powers of analysis, if you allow yourself to think that what you're creating together is art, then that creation achieves more gravitas, and you can all use your best intelligence in order to help create your piece of art. If you imagine that your fellow players (and the audience) are your equals instead of your competition, you give yourself permission to honor your own contribution as well as theirs. It's in everyone's best interest to build the tower as high as we can, using all of our available resources, including all the intelligence and experience that we have.

My students at Menlo put on shows in front of an audience, whereas these games are meant to help you play games with your students all together in a small group. Regardless, the mantra, "See what's happening; help it happen," still applies to both the teaching and the learning. As teachers sometimes we have the impulse to over-explain an activity, hoping to fast-track through it by pointing out the common mistakes ahead of time so that our students won't make them and will therefore be "good at it" that much faster. However, when we set up such specific expectations for an open-ended activity like playing an improv game, the students now have a pre-existing framework that they didn't create. They may therefore become overly concerned with comparing what's actually happening to what's "supposed to happen." This is why in improv class I like to slightly under-explain exercises, so that students are forced to

---

4   *Truth in Comedy*, p. 43. (One of Del Close's teaching mantras that's oft-repeated by improv teachers.)

try them and merely see what's *actually* happening, and respond in the way that seems most obvious to them in the moment. I know that I, as a very experienced improvisor, have a certain expectation of how a game or exercise will go — but I'd much rather be surprised by what actually happens. The students can "help it happen" by building off of what's being created in the present moment, and you can "help it happen" by pointing out and describing the work that everyone, students and teachers, is experiencing as it unfolds. If you point out the roadblocks and "teachable moments" that your PRESENT students encountered, rather than some long-ago students that live only in your memory, it's much more applicable to the current situation.

Each of us has a set of abilities, experience, assumptions, and knowledge that we carry around with us all the time. Those tools are all inside our heads, however. They become visible in the ways we use them, but are otherwise invisible to everyone else. When a group is beginning something new, whether it's an improvised story or a group project, the way to use the mantra, "See what's happening; help it happen," is to imagine that everyone's looking at the same blank space. At the beginning, nothing has been created. Then someone adds something. Maybe it's the first sentence of a story, or a first idea for a project. Now everyone can see that one first thing. Each using our own set of tools, we think of an instant storm of possible connections. Someone adds a second thing. Now we look at our new world, consisting of these two things. We reevaluate. What's happening now? How has this world changed? How can I help it now? Some of the connections we made a split second ago are no longer relevant and therefore no longer helpful. Some of them are *more* relevant! Someone adds a third thing. What's happening now, and how can we help? Working with my best intelligence, how can I add the thing that will be the most helpful in this moment?

Every new project starts empty. Whatever may be going on inside our heads, the only things that appear in the new project are the things we actually contribute. Before we contribute, we look and ask ourselves, Is this going to help? If it might help later, keep it in your pocket. If it's probably not going to help, toss it. If you're telling a story and someone's named the kingdom already, naming the kingdom again with an "even better name" is not going to be helpful, so no matter what your great kingdom name is, let it go for now (or remember it for a future story). If you think, "Maybe this kingdom is the kind that would get attacked by a dragon at some point," keep that in your pocket — you might get to use it. Every step becomes easier if you just look at what's happening and do the thing that seems to you like it should come next.

ON PLAYING GAMES

OK, If I'm Going To Lead These Games, What Do I Need To Know?

If you're a teacher or a parent, aiming to have improv-type interactions with a child yourself, or to facilitate improv-type games and interactions between children, you've got to keep in mind that you've got built-in high status (we'll talk more about that later). It's not your fault; it's the way things are already set up! But because of that, you're going to be accustomed to controlling situations, and the children in question are likely accustomed to that as well, and will by default look to you for guidance, approval, and behavioral precedent. "Leading the activity" is a project in itself, and as such, the language and behavior you contribute to it are affecting the process just as much as playing the game. Therefore, in situations where your students are improvising, your job is not only to look for opportunities to help the children understand the process and their own participation, but also to keep an eye on your own behavior so that you're also interacting with them according to the principles of improv. Even while you're coaching, facilitating or playing, see what's happening.

Everyone Should Play

Depending on your particular situation, you might well be playing these games in a situation where there are others present who don't feel like playing. They might be parents of the kids who are playing, or they might be other kids who aren't interested in participating, or they might be other types of bystanders. For the purposes of these exercises, I strongly urge you to either coax those people into playing with you, or else move either them or yourselves to another place. When you're trying to play improv games with the intent to create a safe place and discover failure together, the last thing you need is an audience of people who feel too cool to participate, but cool enough to watch and make comments. Any comments are unhelpful, even a well-meaning "Good job, honey!" from someone's parent. As the Heisenberg Uncertainty Principle states, observation changes the thing it's observing;[1] merely the knowledge that there's an outside audience can change behavior within the group. Any audience-oriented behavior in these group improv situations can be directly counterproductive: an audience can reward someone with laughter for behavior that's ultimately unhelpful to the group (see "Practicing knocking down the tower"). We'd like the group's energy to be directed productively towards each other, not laugh-seeking towards an uninvolved audience. Therefore, as the facilitator, it's definitely worth your effort to remove the element of an uninvolved audience, either by incorporating them into the group of players, or by putting physical distance between players and outside observers.

If the outsiders are parents of children in your group, you can kindly explain that their children will teach them these games later, but that they

---

[1] It's true about physics and quantum-level particles, but it's also true about humans.

can't watch if they're not going to play; right now the games are for the group and they would like to play without an audience.[2] If the outsiders are children who are in your group and should be participating with you but are choosing not to, you can merely focus your positive attention on the children participating, and treat as uninteresting any disruptive behaviors of those who aren't, and the outliers will hopefully soon come round and start participating, without anyone making a big deal of it.

Dealing With Your Own Status

If you're an adult, playing games with children, or if you've given yourself the status of "facilitator" in any kind of group at all, make sure you pay extra attention to the group dynamic. All the notes you would give players, about cooperation and building together, apply equally to you. Especially if you're not someone who's taken an improv class before (You should! It's fun!), do remember that the instincts you carry with you are deeply ingrained. Therefore, if you find yourself having any of these reactions outlined further along in this section, remember: it's not your fault! This is totally normal stuff to be thinking and feeling. A lot of the process of learning improv is the difficult process of remembering what it was like to be a small child, when fantasy and reality were much closer together, and scary things were all more or less imaginary. Kids are naturally creative and have that improvisor talent of saying things that might sound off-the-wall, but come from a place of logic; in their

---

2   And if you wind up playing with other parents playing with kids, you make sure that you give them the same exact hints and sidecoaching that you would one of the children... kids notice unfairness above all else.

creation, they typically need guidance and trust-building, in order to be constructive and work together.[3]

When I speak of "status" in an improv context, I'm referring to interpersonal status. Someone who's "high status" basically feels as if they have a disproportionately high degree of control over a given situation.[4] Especially where children are concerned, the functions adults perform have a lot to do with status and safety. And because adults naturally also have higher status than kids (being usually older, larger, and/or louder), they're used to their opinion being the most important one. Adults can also learn a lot from acknowledging their own assumptions and unlearning a lot of ingrained instincts. When adults are improvising with each other, the status tends to balance itself out somewhat, because other adults know how to push back, and adults recognize the status of other adults. But an adult among children will have status effects both intentional and unintentional… it's wise to recognize when you're accidentally controlling a situation, so that you can work on only doing it when you mean to, and when it's necessary for the activity, and not just because you're the adult and you feel like maintaining arbitrary control *within* an activity.

Parent/teacher high status can manifest itself in a couple of ways. One of them is controlling the story itself. When storytelling, try to resist the following (again, perfectly natural) control reactions. If you and a child are creating a story together, or you are moderating while children

---

[3] The following study examined cooperation in very young children, and how they reflected the general human tendencies to share and cooperate with close relations, with people who've shared with them, and with people they know have shared with others (Olson, Kristina R. and Elizabeth S. Spelke, "Foundations of cooperation in young children," ScienceDirect, 2007.)

[4] Keith Johnstone wrote extensively about status, and I base my definitions on his writings and teachings. For more on status, see the appendix.

create a story, you might think to yourself, "Wait! I'm an adult, I know better!" You might have these automatic reactions:

- You might be tempted to say, "No, that's not what happens; I have a better idea."
- You might be tempted to say, "Ok, that happens, but then this terrible thing happens as a result!"
- You might be tempted to say, "Okayyyyyy, but when something bad happens, I'm going to say I told you so!"
- You might be tempted to say, "Really? That's never going to work."
- You might be tempted to say, "Are you sure? That idea's weird."

As you might be able to tell, reading them, these reflexes mostly stem from anxiety over being in control of a situation. But a story isn't real, and things in story worlds don't have the same consequences as they might in the real world. It's OK for things to happen in a story that seem weird or dangerous. In fact, it's hard for stories to happen if nothing weird or dangerous happens. (Kids don't really like stories in which nothing bad ever happens or at least threatens to happen …) It's even OK for a story you're creating to just plain turn out so terrible or confusing that you don't even make it to the end. So if you have these reactions, try to notice and then suppress them, in favor of "Sure, why not!"[5] We can learn from a story that gets confusing, tragic, and/or boring; it's OK to let it get there.

---

5   The one sticky point is that authority figures are often responsible, in some cases, legally, for censoring out gross/disgusting/sexual/violent/mean language. Kids tell stories about poop and pee and people being naked and all sorts of things, and people dying and getting eaten and stuff, because they think that's funny. But it's odd that mostly people dying and getting eaten is usually OK, whereas poop and pee and naked-type stuff is usually shut down … go figure, in this prudish culture.

Another way parent/teachers can accidentally wield their status is in a moderator vein, handing down arbitrary judgment between players. "*You* did it right and *you* did it wrong," or "So-and-so's idea is better, let's do that." If something's not working between players, it might seem faster to just declare what the problem is, or quickly decide who was in the wrong. It's more helpful to let the players involved figure it out by asking what they think is happening. If one idea is better for a specific reason (the other one is offensive or violent, for example), explain your thoughts as someone whose job it is to keep everyone safe. And if there's simply a clash of opposing ideas, see if you can help them make everyone's idea right.

Often, when I'm working with theater students and I tell kids to get together in groups and quickly plan something, I'll look around the room and see one or two kids from a group sulking off to the side, and when I investigate, it turns out these kids' ideas didn't pass muster with the rest of their group. This happened recently at an elementary school program I teach at. When I went to investigate, the little girls said, "We wanted to all be kitties, but he wants to be a ninja." I said, "Can we do something that uses both ideas?" Just saying that was enough to have the kitties say, "Oh. What if we're kitties and the ninja comes and scares us?" and then boom, everyone was happy and productive and involved in the story. The goal is for all the kids to feel included and have a role to play, and to help them realize that just because you didn't expect someone's idea, it doesn't mean it won't work with yours.

As adults, we feel a lot of pressure to be doing things right all the time, right away, whether we've done them or not, and we tend to project this pressure onto smaller people too. We're pretty scared of doing new things, sometimes. What if we're bad at them? What will the kids think of me then? As adults, we have to be careful when learning this craft together with children, not to bulldoze their ideas in the attempt to have them "do it right," right now, right away ... kids often do this jumping-right-in kind of thing right already. What you want them to learn is how to pay attention and be nice to each other along the way; if they're not listening or they're being non-constructive, you can help them see how and why — but if they're just coming up with ideas you don't like or think are weird, that's not necessarily "doing it wrong," so redirecting them in that case is just confusing and counterproductive.

The practice of improv is about giving and taking, in every moment: letting people gently control each other, learning to be OK with the other person being the boss sometimes. The flip side is, when you're being the boss in that moment, you want the other person to be having a good time, so that they want to play with you ... So, you should probably not do things that make them go away or that are mean or hurt their bodies or their feelings.

(Also, in a more structured situation where you're a grownup who has declared yourself to be the "leader," do be careful that you aren't taking over their games just because you think they're awfully fun ... you want to teach them to lead each other, which sometimes means allowing them to lead you ... allow yourself to be just one of the players sometimes.)

If These Are Games, How Come I Can't Win Them?

A lot of group games for children, games that I see played at places like camps, are often competitive and elimination-based. Now, there's nothing wrong with the idea of competitive games per se; many popular improvised performance formats are based on competition, such as Keith Johnstone's TheatreSports™, Micetro™, and Gorilla Theater™; or ComedySportz™. Within these formats, and in other kinds of improv shows, there are plenty of games that result in people "losing" or getting eliminated. The difference in my mind is that these are performance formats, and that having someone win is a frame for the show. The performers themselves know that it doesn't mean that the winner is better than the others. As professionals, they put on these shows and play these games frequently, and have plenty of practice winning some and losing some. (And shhhh, sometimes if the show needs it they even lose *on purpose*.)

But in other informal situations, where performance is not part of the situation, groups play these games for fun, and unfortunately sometimes the ones that they play for "fun" set up an antagonistic relationship within the group, where playing the game correctly means being directly annoying or mean-spirited towards the other players. This has a tendency to reward exclusionary behavior, further separating those who are "joiners" and those who are "loners." Winning at these kinds of games also directly rewards thinking up ways to be annoying, tricky, or otherwise antagonistic. There's nothing wrong with elimination games per se, but I find that in many environments, the way those games are played and used, in structured or unstructured situations, emphasize the power of exclusion: they accidentally reinforce "cool kids (and teacher)" versus "bad kids who are bad at things." *I'm* interested in pointing out and deconstructing for the kids the very concept of status, which means noticing and pointing out when people are made to feel small, instead of pretending that since most of us are happy, everyone's happy.

When playing elimination games in a large group, once you become eliminated, the focus is off you. It feels like you've been discarded. No one is paying attention to you any longer, because they're still all focused on the potential winners. The bigger the group, the longer you're expected to sit and cheer for those still in the running. What you accidentally learn from that is that once you're eliminated, you become worthless. No one really cares what you do anymore during this time, or even whether you pay attention to the rest of the game. Either that, or you are made to sit still and stare at the competition going on without you, a competition in which you no longer have any stake. And those still in the game also learn that those who are eliminated are worthless; therefore, it becomes really really important to never ever fail. That may sound like a ridiculously dire account of what it feels like to play a silly game, but even when the game is over, even if the game is trivial, the feeling lingers. Its effects are disproportionate and cumulative. Especially since in most situations there's no effort made to deconstruct what happened in the game; someone won, that's what's important.

If no one loses, it also doesn't mean that everyone wins at these games in the way that people complain about the concepts of grade inflation and overcomplimenting and everyone getting a trophy. (There are studies also that show that kids who are just told "you're good at that!" will actually become worse, whereas kids who are told "you worked hard to do that!" will constantly be improving.[6]) I'm not aiming for blanket approval any more than I'm aiming for blanket criticism.[7] I want everyone to learn that they're working on developing *skills*, and that they should be congratulated for improvement, for *trying* and failing and trying again at something they're getting better at — not just for flawless ease. I don't mind elimination games, as long as they don't end up teaching the players that one failure is the end of the road, and by

---

6   It's a subject I see popping up in studies and blogs all over the place; I'm citing a post by Peggy Drexler, Ph.D on the Psychology Today blog, "The key to raising confident kids? Stop complimenting them!" (https://www.psychologytoday.com/blog, Aug. 17, 2012) It's about creating that "growth mindset." Psychoanalyst Steven Grosz just wrote a book called *The Examined Life*, wherein he talks about praise being detrimental. Scientists from Singapore and the US just completed four studies of college students in Hong Kong and the US, which held that students rating their own performance as higher than it actually was, were more depressed than those who rated their performance more accurately.

7   ("What a terrible blanket!" Ahaha.)

extension that failure is their ultimate fate. I want to close the distance between the "winners" and the "losers" so that the people who end up "losing" don't feel like winning is therefore now and forever out of their grasp. I want them to learn that winning is achievable, and losing isn't terrible and unbearable.

Kids sometimes say, "But it's no fun if no one wins." Well, sure. Maybe it's fun if someone wins, if that person is you. And if you've been taught to judge your own prowess just in terms of winning. But I'm interested in inclusion; I'm interested in challenging the valuing of individual winning above all else. As far as most of these games are concerned, when the game is going well and everyone's playing it and having fun, then everybody wins together. Winning means successful cooperation. Kids, especially younger kids, sometimes find it harder to work together and include everyone, so that's the thing that's more valuable to work on.

But wasn't I talking about failure not too long ago? It's definitely true: everyone needs to learn how to be a good loser; not everyone can win a soccer game, or a spelling bee, or the lottery. Not everyone can get into the college they apply for, or get the job they want. But they need to be familiar enough with casual "failure" of silly, unimportant things that when something *actually* important goes wrong, they don't fall apart. What they need to practice is not the losing itself, but the losing and feeling *cheerful* about it.[8] When you're shamed for failing at something, even if it's in jest, you learn that failure is shameful. You learn that you should avoid failure at all costs, and should refuse to own up to any errors you've made. But when there's a big celebration every time someone messes up, failure loses its sting.

---

8   To cite just one source, see the online article "The Science of Failure: Why Highly Successful People Crave Mistakes." *https://blog.bufferapp.com/why-highly-successful-people-crave-failure-and-mistakes*

When we play a game like **Statues**,[9] or **Sheep und Wolf**[10], or any game where kids have to "catch" each other, I like to remind them that the game is about being brave and testing the limits. Playing it safe means you may never be caught and tagged, but then you probably won't have much fun. When kids are caught moving by the Statues museum guard, I congratulate them for being so brave and taking such a big risk. When kids are eliminated from games, I often have them take a bow, and sometimes have the other kids clap for them, if the gameplay accommodates that. The important thing is not the winning or the losing, but the ability to cheerfully (and accurately) identify when you've won, and when you've lost.

I'm an advocate of games where you can mess up and there's an immediate mini-consequence, but then you can keep playing. That way, everyone can see that the "rules" of the game are being followed, and everyone can also keep practicing, honing their skills at following those particular rules. In games usually played with eliminations, you might instead have people do a "forfeit": some silly thing like doing a dance, making a gesture, taking a bow, or finding a new place in the. You could also have everyone do something when someone makes an error, maybe yell and scatter to new positions in the circle. Whatever it is, we're acknowledging that, oops, someone failed at something, and that's cool; now they can start again.

Facilitator Fundamentals: See What's Happening

As a facilitator, the most important thing is to *pay attention* to what's going on. Really pay attention. Just like an improvisor who's planning

---

9   See page 201
10 See page 241

too much, if you spend all your time thinking of what you're going to say or do next in your class, you'll miss the valuable things that are actually happening, whether they're teachable moments or innovations that are surprising and wonderful.

It's especially important when you're facilitating in a group to keep an eye on the secret and sometimes nonverbal behavior that's going on. Are kids being nice to each other, or are they using their bodies or their words to exclude or hurt others? (Is no one choosing to sit next to a certain kid, for example?) When things like that happen, it's often because kids think that "no one can see them." If a teacher's talking, they think a teacher's also blind. Weird, right? They think that because they're trying to be secretive, they're actually succeeding at being secretive. However, I always point out to kids that "if you're onstage, the audience can see you." This remains true in a small group. I wonder if it's because kids can't see themselves, so they assume no one else can see them either. This leads to not only antisocial behavior but also funny things such as picking their noses and scratching their butts. They don't really realize that people can actually see them.[11]

If something's going on outside the exercise at hand that's clearly disrupting the group dynamic, it's a good idea to nip it in the bud, and demonstrate (either subtly or overtly) that you can, in fact, see what's going on.

If something wonky is going on *inside* the exercise at hand, it's great to point out where things went really well, and also where things went awry. It's also good to talk to them about whether they recognize the constructive and non-constructive things that are happening. It's good to

---

11   There is a science of peekaboo. Cambridge scientists completed a study in 2012 which concluded that most very small children likely believe that if no one can see their eyes or make eye contact with them, it means they're invisible. (*Daily Mail,* 2014 "Peekaboo! Cambridge scientists discover why children think they are invisible when they hide their eyes")

reinforce their own confidence in their own powers of observation; kids see *everything*, and they want you to notice.[12]

Facilitator Fundamentals: Help it Happen

In the case of facilitating, the thing you want to help happen is either: the thing you planned, *or* the thing that whatever you've planned has become. Huh? Crazy!

Sometimes while playing a game, things get a little scattered, or kids are embarrassed or confused (or *you* get confused) and the game gets sidetracked. In those cases, it's a good idea to actually name what you're seeing. You can just say, "Gosh, that went wrong, didn't it?", demonstrate commitment to the exercise, and suggest you all try it again, with*out* exerting too much overt status. ("You have to do it because I'm making you" is not a terribly productive way to get kids to participate.) You can try again to help it happen.

But you can also continue to see what's happening. If they're embarrassed or confused or uncertain, that doesn't come from nowhere. They're legitimately feeling strange for some reason, and that's OK. It's time to reassess: does the game need to be re-explained and clarified? Do they need a demonstration first? Do they just feel silly? In the latter case, I acknowledge their feelings, and tell them, "If it makes you feel silly, you're on the right track! It's weird, you're right. That's the point!" I also acknowledge another potential kind of feeling, especially for those who are too-cool-for-school: "It's OK to make fun of it while you're doing it, as long as you also do it." Especially for kids who are new to theater, I

---

[12] Kids also want you to notice when they're doing something they shouldn't be doing. Something that seems to work, when acknowledging but also discouraging certain behavior, which I learned from preschool teachers: saying, "No thank you."

just keep naming what's happening: "Yep, it's totally weird. And that's OK." Depending on their age, kids are more or less afraid of looking weird in front of their peers. And in the end, if they're uncomfortable with the game or it's not a good fit for them, what's been happening might in fact be halfway to playing another game, instead. If you see that happening, you can just tweak the current exercise to fit the existing situation, and then, boom! Success!

SKILLS FOR EVERYONE

The Section of This Book That's About Playing With Others

When you're having improv time, there's a range of creative activities to try. There are games that involve showing off goofy things for each other. There are also activities that are primarily verbal or storytelling-related. You could try activities that are mostly physical or entirely nonverbal. And then there are games that are meant to be played as warm-ups or just to be enjoyed in a circle by the participants. There are even activities that translate improv to other media, such as writing or drawing. All of these count as improvising, creating using the tools of the improvisor, but they're diverse enough to fit a variety of moods and temperaments. Some of them can be played in pairs or groups and sometimes even alone … there are drawings and paintings and music … things loud and quiet; things rambunctious and still … the point of them all is to learn to listen and build, to have fun by working together.

These games represent some ways to incorporate improvisational activities and imaginative play into their daily routines, without the pressures of being "onstage." Some of the games presented, however, are more successful when there are others watching and waiting to take their turn, either for learning purposes or for mere audience/focus purposes.

Other activities are suitable for groups of any size, down to two people playing a game just for fun or to pass the time (in the car, while waiting in line …).

A note on "games" …

As described earlier, most of these games aren't games you can "win" at… so why are they called games? Well, many improv gurus talk about "finding the game" in a scene, and that's often more what a game is. What does that mean? Well, it's basically about finding something that happens twice.

The simplest game ever, and an example of "finding the game":

I like to play this with shy babies; it's about as simple a game as you can have. Make some eye contact, inhale expectantly with a big grin, and then touch them on the hand and say "Boop!" Wait for a reaction, then… do it again![1] Now it's happened twice! Try it a third time; you'll probably get laughter. Things in threes are funny! It's a game! Now that you've both got the hang of it, you can try varying it, by "breaking" the rules you just created: maybe one time you wait longer between the breath and the boop. Maybe you boop them on the other hand, or maybe the nose! Maybe the forehead! It's quite likely, given the appropriate motor skills, that the shy baby will try to boop you back, or even boop someone else. This game has some set parameters that define it as the game you're playing; you're poking someone while saying "boop." It wouldn't be the same game without those two rules. But no one wins this game; it's just

---

[1] To build some extra suspense, or to reassure an incredibly shy baby, try unengaging for a few moments between turns, to demonstrate that you're not being overly aggressive or invasive.

fun. You can escalate it until the point where it feels like it's over, but no single participant "wins."

The point of improv-style games is not to get really good at performing improv games. (That's another good reason not to play them only for performance; audience approval isn't the primary goal.) The goal is for the games to make you do things you're not used to doing, or don't want to, and for the result to surprise and delight you. The goal is not really to be good at doing it "right," the goal is to prod you into surprising yourself. All of these games train for the same overlapping sets of skills of paying attention, trusting yourself, trusting your partners, and being constructive, so that's what you're *really* getting good at, when you play improv games. By emphasizing the rules of the game, you're secretly training all the other skills involved, upon which you are *not* putting pressure ... and by not overemphasizing the performance of those skills directly, you're allowing players to self-select what's working and what's not working.

Clive Barker, in *Theater Games*, writes:

> "Children's games and play are a very complicated area of human activity, and psychologists are right to remind us that the child is not just a small adult. Nor is he the simple blank page on which an adult character will later be writ large. He is a human being in the process of learning by experimentation. Mobility is one important part of his learning. Through games, the child explores the range of movement possibilities open to him. He tests his progress by leaping at tree branches, jumping streams, walking on walls. He devises often quite complicated structures for developing control over his movement, and perfecting skills."[2]

---

2   *Theatre Games*, p.63

Barker writes here specifically about movement, but the same experimentation applies to other skills: drawing, vocabulary, rhyming, anything you can imagine that a child may be capable of."

I remember reading in a book about teaching theater, though can't now for the life of me find where, that the point when a game becomes interesting is after the point when it becomes boring.[3] You need to do it enough to get good at it, and then for it to feel just slightly tedious, and then past that point, in order to discover the second level of stuff in it. It's not about being good at playing the game, but finding something interesting and fun while you happen to be playing it. Just when you start to assume that you've got it all figured out, that's when you really start learning something new. Another way to think about it is, when you've got it figured out, you've figured out the limitations of the game's stated (or hidden) rules, just like the baby figures out the rules of "boop!" In further iterations, you can therefore begin to explore all the ways in which to try and break those rules. Play the game a few more times and try to "break" it. In practice, this means that you should probably try something at least two or three times before you give up or decide you "don't like it." If it's "a little too hard," that's the best reason to keep playing it! If it's "way too hard," try coming back to it later.

Another thing about games, that piggybacks off that same sentiment: Some of these games are easier for younger children to play than others, *but* every improv-style game that younger children can play, can and should be played by absolutely everyone older than the minimum age for comprehension. Just like a game is only interesting after it's "boring," adults can get a lot out of a game, even/especially if on the surface it seems silly or dumb. If part of what we're doing in playing these games is cutting back to the wonder, then of course we want to play games

---

[3] Was it in *Theatre Games*? Or Peter Brooks' *The Empty Space*? Of course now I can't find it.

that small children could also play. Most of these games I learned from adults, who were teaching other adults. If you think you already know everything you need to know about a game, that just means you're making prescriptive assumptions, something that adults definitely do. Reading a game description that looks intriguing or fun or stupid? Try it … you might like it!

A STARTER KIT

Some Things To Know and Remember

Some vocabulary:

Facilitator:

When I use the term "facilitator," what I really mean is, "The person who's decided they're going to teach these games to someone else." They're the "point person," the one who's read the instructions. Really, it requires no more expertise than that. I find that often, when I'm playing a board or card game with a group of people, there's someone who either knows the rules already (if they've played it before), or someone who decides they're going to read the rules and keep track of them during gameplay, to the best of their knowledge (if no one has played it before). Certainly, in a table game situation, the facilitator is in all other ways just a regular player: The only difference is, they have one eye on the rulebook.

For the purposes of this book, I'm operating with a similar assumption. Depending on the specific situation and location, the facilitator may be supervising a group while not playing a game themselves, or they may desire to be just another player in the group. Either way, the facilitator should assume that their job is to make gameplay easier for everyone else, while assuming that the rules of the game also apply to everyone including themselves.

Game:

Defining this is actually kind of philosophical! Webster's online dictionary defines "game" as either an "activity engaged in for diversion or amusement: play" or "a procedure or strategy for gaining an end: tactic."

Dictionary.com describes a game as "a competitive activity involving skill, chance, or endurance on the part of two or more persons who play according to a set of rules, usually for their own amusement or for that of spectators."

The word "game" in improv has two interrelated meanings, both of which are found in these definitions. The first meaning is the more common one that describes the "games" or exercises in this book, wherein I set out the rules and describe how to play. In this case, a "game" is something you do for amusement, something that has rules, and that can either be played just for fun, or to delight onlookers.

The "procedure or strategy" is the part of the definition that refers to "The Game," in the sense of "find the game." The rules describe the game as exercise, and "the game" describes the procedure, the strategy, the WAY you might play it, as it develops. For example, you might choose to play the game/exercise Red Ball. As you're playing, however, you might notice that you've started saying "Red ball!" in silly voices, and that's the "Game" that develops organically ... you just created a game within the game. If you continue to develop and explore these silly voices, you're playing the game (Red Ball) while also playing The Game.

Improvisors use the same word to describe both things, and… well, it's just confusing. Welcome to the fun world of making up your own rules!

Stage:

The bubble where theater happens. This book isn't big on performance games, but sometimes things do take place "onstage," and the rule about the stage is that the people who aren't onstage probably shouldn't intrude with voice or body onto the stage… by doing so, they're making themselves a part of the scene.

Scene:

Anything that happens in the magical bubble that is "theater time." A scene is anything that takes place in the world of the stage, within its boundaries and inside stage time, where the normal reality is replaced by "stage reality" and the onlookers are not part of it. It's like a scene from a play. Not all games are "scenes" (ball games are not scenes) and not all scenes start with the rules of a game.

To reinforce the bubble of theater time, I recommend that you pick a set of signals to use consistently, to designate when a scene is happening and the audience should pay attention and not interact with the people onstage, and when the scene is over and the audience can interact again. I use "lights up" and "lights down"; you can use "action!" and "scene!" or "curtain!" and "blackout!" or anything else that makes sense to you.

Offer:

Anything that's conjured into existence by the improvisors. Could be an idea, a suggestion, an actual object. An offer is anything that adds to the reality of the scene; it's like a building block in your tower. Maybe it's integral to the support of your tower, or maybe it's just decorative — but once it's created, it exists.

Accept:

You "accept" an offer by validating its reality. "Mom!" someone might say to you to when starting a scene. "Yes, dear," you reply as Mom, thus accepting the offer that you are, indeed, the mom in the scene. Or you might say, "Young man, where have you been!" which also accepts the offer that you are, in fact, the mom — and you're also adding that a certain young man is home late and may be in Big Trouble.

Blocking:

Also referred to by some improvisors as "denial," blocking is the opposite of accepting. Replying to "Mom!" with "Nope, I'm not your mom!" is blocking or denying the offer. You're knocking down the tower.

Sidecoach:

Where it says "sidecoach" in the text, what it means is simply this: "sidecoaching" is the practice of making helpful suggestions *while* an exercise is happening — while the players are on their feet in the middle of the game — so that you can steer the activity instead of stopping it. You can give tips as close in time as possible to the "teachable moment" in order to maximize retention. Using sidecoaching, you can even pause, "erase," and replay a moment, in order to immediately have the players apply a change. It's often more effective to have them implement a change and see what happens right away, than it is to tell them after the fact, "Well, that was okay, but next time try this instead." Make this time "next time."

Sidecoaching Reminders:

Handy things to say, to keep everyone on track

- **"See what's happening; help it happen."** Just repeating either or both of these clauses can remind people to keep their eyes open, observe the present moment, and be constructive with their offers.
- **Hold on tightly; let go lightly.** (It's the main character's motto in the film *Croupier*, though the quote comes originally from a John Denver song.[1]) What do I mean by this? It's important to commit to your own ideas, and not discard them. On the other hand, if the time for your idea is past or it otherwise just doesn't quite fit anymore, poof! it's OK to let it go.
- **Whoever defines it first is right.** When we're building something together by improvising, we start from nothing and build using only what everyone can see and hear. Even if you had a different idea in your head that you hadn't contributed yet, whatever choice actually gets made has by definition become the right choice, because it's the one everyone can see or hear.

---

[1] "Hold On Tightly," off the album *It's About Time* (1983).

Keith Johnstone wrote: "The improviser has to be like a man walking backwards. He sees where he has been, but he pays no attention to the future."[2] Therefore: What's happened already is true. As in my earlier example, if someone's already named the kingdom, that kingdom has been NAMED. Whatever that name is, it's by definition the right one.
- **Find the game.** If you're looking for direction within a story or a scene, see what's happening. Has anything happened twice? (Or is someone doing anything fun or interesting enough that you'd *like* it to happen twice?) See if you can get it to happen again, and make that your game!

Other Sidecoach Notes: Things to keep in mind.

- **Use a pretend name!** Teach children to call each other by imaginary names, not their real names, when they're playing characters. Made-up names will help reinforce that everything that's happening is pretend, and that no one is playing themselves. It will make it easier for children to embody characters that are very unlike themselves: different genders, different emotions, different physicalities, different opinions. It will also make it easier for children to let each other play those different characters, if they're used to assuming that everything, even names, are pretend.
- **Make your partner look good/Give your partner a good time**: When we play improv games, we're trusting each

---

2 *Impro*, p. 116.

other. Help build that trust by playing nice: your partner is instructed to be cooperative and constructive — but on the other hand, be nice to your partner by being aware of what they will enjoy cooperating with. If you expect your partner to say yes to your offer, offer something they'll like. As Spiderman says, "With great power comes great responsibility." If you can make someone do something else, it's your responsibility to make sure that it's something that's OK with the other person — not the CHARACTER they're playing, but the person inside.

- **It's a safe place**: Especially with groups of kids, a facilitator has to be vigilant in order to make sure that they're really being nice to each other, in the beginning… inside jokes and things like that might pop up, or real people might be used as suggestions. Try to steer them away from things like that, even (or especially) if they don't think there's any harm in it; until the group is really solidified as one friendly, comfortable, safe group, it's easy for them to alienate each other, whether it's on purpose or by accident (one kid's friendly banter is another kid's mean-spirited teasing, and kids can't always tell when they're actually hurting someone's feelings).

- **Admit when *you've* made a mistake about something**: If there were "rules" or conditions that you stated, that have been violated for whatever reason, you just need to apologize for it. No need to justify why it was a good idea anyway and you did nothing wrong… it's better to say, "Oops! You're right, I'm sorry," and then offer a way to fix it, if necessary.

The number of children you're playing with may vary widely, from one child to hundreds.[3] Still, you as a facilitator should assume that the rules of improv apply equally to you, whether you're playing a specific game or not.

---

[3] Thanks to AAUW's Tech Trek Program, I've given improv workshops to 120+ kids at once, on the front lawn of a college residence.. It's possible … as long as you have a loud voice.

PART THREE:

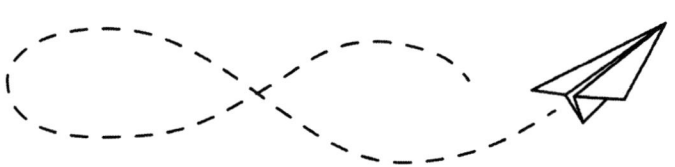

MISCHIEF

GAMES FOR SEEING WHAT'S HAPPENING

As I see it, a facilitator who's reading the rules in order to make it easier for others to play, should first try to absorb the statements and philosophies in the previous chapters. In a structured improv situation, the next step is to run the players through some fundamentals. In any kind of structured or planned improv progression, it's useful for players to work through the exercises in this chapter; as Yoda put it, "You must unlearn what you have learned." The games in this section may only be useful once ever, and that's okay. Their job is to create "teachable moments," to jog players into thinking constructively, to guide them into what it might mean to see what's happening and help it happen.

You as a facilitator may only need to run your players through these first three exercises once, ever — and that's fine. Hopefully, they make their impact, and that's the point. These exercises are designed to create a certain strangeness, to make the world a little unfamiliar and thus new again. The students (and possibly you) may be confused, but working through this confusion and out the other side is part of the process. Explaining these first few exercises too much beforehand defeats the purpose; among other things, it's creating a precedent that you don't need to be an expert at something before trying it for the first time.

Concept One: Being Constructive

(Seeing what's happening and helping it happen)

A very basic reflex most of us have, which has kept us as a species from going extinct, is to say NO to things that seem dangerous, scary, unknown, or unexpected. "Hey, hear that growling outside the cave? Let's go see what it is!" "No thanks." Guess which one gets eaten, and which carries their genetic material forward. Caution is ingrained in our behavior.

Saying NO also happens to be a quick and easy way to exert control over a situation, which also helps us feel safer. "Let's try a new restaurant!" "No." "OK, let's go ice fishing!" "No. " "Well… how about volcano surfing?" "Nope." "Can I borrow your pencil, then?" "Nope." As you can see, some of these are dangerous activities, and some are fairly reasonable requests. But sometimes we lose the power to tell the difference. Saying no can bring all kinds of activities to a screeching halt! We won't get hurt OR look silly! The power is intoxicating!

There are some sneaky workarounds that your brain might try, when being weaned to say yes instead of no. There's the nefarious (and passive-aggressive) "yes, but," which has the power to SOUND constructive but still tone down or even entirely cancel the offer being "accepted."

A: Let's go to the zoo!

B: Ok, but it closes in ten minutes.

Person B seems to be agreeing to the activity, while still controlling the fact that it will stop soon.

A: Did you bring the radio?

B: Yes, but it's broken.

Once again, person B accepts the offer, and cancels it, in the same sentence. Sneaky! Still not getting anywhere. Let's try accepting:

A: Did you bring the radio?

B: Yep.

Er... closer, but still not being constructive. Accepting the offer and still not adding anything new isn't being DEstructive, but it's not being CONstructive, either. Let's try again:

A: Did you bring the radio?

B: Yes, and listen, I'm picking up their signal!

Aha! Person B, now you're accepting the offer AND adding onto it constructively! Well done.

Why are we so good at saying no?

Of course, some real-life activities have the potential to cause actual physical harm, and those are pretty good to say no to. In a playtime or storytelling situation, however, there's usually no real physical danger involved in a suggestion. You can easily *pretend* to try a new restaurant, go ice fishing, or practice your volcano surfing without fear of being real-life injured (unless you're clumsy). So, why on earth not say yes to a pretend suggestion?

As for looking silly, that's a little more difficult to overcome. We spend a lot of time being afraid that we're embarrassing ourselves: with what we wear, what we say, how we look, even what we think. The logical conclusion there is that most everyone else is also thinking that about themselves, all the time. The result is that no one is as concerned with what you're doing as *you* are, and that if you just go about your business, people will be incredibly impressed with your confidence. Yes, people can be really mean to each other. But if someone throws an insult your way, an improv-trained brain can see that it's their tactic for keeping *themselves* safe; they're saying "no" to whatever you have that makes them uncomfortable, in order to stop it from — what, rubbing off on them? Something unexpected that you happen to be doing, saying, or wearing has no direct effect on an uninvolved observer, except to make them jealous that they themselves are scared to deviate from societal expectations. If someone wields ridicule or shame like a weapon, it probably means that they themselves fear ridicule and shame. In an improv environment, everyone is learning to make each other feel good about being themselves and expressing their thoughts, so being "weird," oddball, or unexpected should be safe, celebrated, and perhaps most importantly, seen as perfectly normal.

When I'm working with my students (especially in the middle-school ranges, ages 10-13), I often tell them, during a silly warmup or other "weird" exercise, "If it makes you feel dumb, you're doing it right!" I also often tell my students that they actually LOOK the silliest when they're not trying very hard. Believe it or not, I'll say, someone trying halfheartedly to dance in a big dance number is going to stand out a lot more than someone fully committing to even the goofiest of dance moves. Acknowledge that it's making you feel silly, and then push beyond that and start having fun, and then you're really doing it right.

A very fundamental thing we're going to practice every time we improvise is to accept other people's offers, and we're also going to try to accept our own. When we say "I can't think of anything!" what we probably mean is, "I've rejected all the things I've thought of and now

I'm stuck." Therefore, try saying the first thing you're thinking of. Even if it seems terrible.[1]

On "Yes," "No," "Construction" and "Destruction"

There's "saying yes," and then there's "being constructive." The whole POINT of saying "yes" is to add material to your creation. You're trying to build something together: a story, a situation, an imaginary room, whatever. It's like building a tower. The temptation to knock down a tower is really, really strong. This plays out quite literally in the case of little kids with blocks. Often small children will spend large amounts of time building towers. Sometimes they knock them over themselves, experimenting with how high the tower can go, and what happens when the tower gets knocked down. However, I'm sure you've noticed that if someone builds a tower with blocks, and someone *else* comes along and gleefully knocks it over, it may be fun for the destroyer, but not really for the builder. "You build a tower, I knock it down" is certainly a game, but it's probably not the game the builder wants to play. The destroyer gets to stay safe, by not having to do any of the building work; they get to do the thing that's "funny," by destroying the tower; they get to "win" the game; and then, they get to walk away, without helping clean up or examining the aftermath. And then, chances are, the builder doesn't particularly feel like playing with the destroyer anymore.

If we settle for construction and then destruction, we might have a very short story indeed. I can't tell you how many word-at-a-time stories I've done with students over the years that are essentially, "Once upon a

---

[1] It might even be a bad word... I mean, it's OK to *think* of a bad word ... your individual environment may dictate whether it's OK to *say* one, though. But at least try not to punish the thought.

time there was a guy and then he died." "Then he died" is certainly an offer, and it's accepting the previous offer: that there was a guy. But it's also not really helpfully building the story, and it's purposefully sending the story to a fiery end. Set up the tower, knock it down, and you have nothing. My high school students, especially the more insecure among them (and who isn't insecure, in high school?), would often sabotage their own endings this way… whether it was a word-at-a-time story, or a scene, they would find some way to make the ending negate or deny or otherwise nullify the rest of the story. For some reason, they couldn't bear to create something without destroying it; they wanted to be able to disown their own creations, cool-person style. (It's a sneaky trick for those that are so inclined: because people are encouraged to say yes to offers, it's tempting to make unconstructive, gross, violent offers because you know they have to be accepted. Also, sometimes it's like a preemptive strike for kids who are shy or who have a negative opinion of themselves: "Everyone hates me! You know I have terrible and stupid ideas! Here, let me prove it! There, see, I knew you'd hate me — let's get it over with! What a terrible idea I just had, right? See? I don't want to play." As long as you don't make it a battle of wills, they'll get over their insecurity and figure out that they can use those creative and mischievous powers in the service of good, instead of to wreak havoc.) It's a very normal reflex, and one that we're going to try to counteract.

Further, the destroyer thinks that just by cancelling the story, they get to end it and walk away, untouched and uninvested. They want to prove, for whatever reason, that they don't *care* about this story they're supposed to be making. Because caring is dumb and embarrassing. But storytellers can also wrangle destruction *into* construction, merely by not stopping once something is destroyed! In any good story, bad things certainly happen to the main characters. Accept and then *over*accept their offered catastrophe. What if the story kept going *after* our guy died? Where did

MANAGED MISCHIEF — GAMES FOR SEEING WHAT'S HAPPENING

he go next? By trying to be destructive in stories, people are trying to be unhelpful, giving up on their own creations — but they're also flirting with exploring disaster, without wanting to make the commitment to examine the aftermath. Stories for children can be saccharine and uneventful, and smart kids know that. They can try to sabotage storylines that they feel are inauthentic, by torpedoing them with ideas that are no doubt from "outside the box." But by working with those torpedoes, you can teach them that the story can be any way they want, and that, yep, those crazy ideas can also be *in*side the box. By keeping the storytelling going through and past a disaster, it may be uncomfortable, but it may also gradually reassure players that they *can* play the game of building alongside everyone else, while still being able to selectively apply narrative catastrophe where it helps serve the story best. They can still have good ideas and play along.

Here are some exercises that will emphasize **SEEING** what's happening. It will teach the act of actually observing what's actually there, and the fact that pointing it out is OK. (The younger the child, the less qualms they'll have about that last bit.) These exercises tend to work best in groups, because you need some people to be **SEEN**, and some people to do the **SEEING**.

Seeing What's Happening: The Super-Basics

This part is kind of like your improv starter kit... a key through the door into the world of improv. In this starter kit, you'll find some useful words to describe what you're doing, some exercises that kick your brain into basic improv gear, and some sidecoach concepts that might function like a Magic 8-ball. If you're stuck, you can consult them and see what happens. They might mean different things to you at different times in your improv journey. You might learn more and more about what they mean as you go. Go through your kit and try everything out, and then wrap it up in your invisible bindle and have fun travelling through the world!

These first three exercises are sort of meta-fundamentals ... they help us SEE what's happening among ourselves, the game-players. Together, they make it okay to notice our own gameplay behavior, and whether we're doing a good job of cooperating and constructing. (As I wrote above: you might only have to do these three exercises on one occasion with a particular group, in order to make the point. But returning to the exercises periodically can be a good refresher course in observation.)

And a bonus: no matter what task you're doing, now or in the future, you can usually make use of the skills these exercises hone: being able to see whether you're being constructive or not, and being able to cheerfully accept failure and move on from it.

Practicing Knocking down the Tower

<u>For: Everyone</u>

In *Impro*, Keith Johnstone talks about "blocking" and accepting offers,[2] and how we can explore those concepts by deliberately practicing just one or the other. "Practicing Knocking Down the Tower" is an exercise in *only* being unconstructive and unhelpful. It can be fun to practice saying no, to really point out how frustrating it can be... and also point a finger at how many different ways there are to say no. (This works to varying degrees of success for varying ages; I've tried this where it's really worked, and I've tried this where the kids just get really confused about what I'm trying to get them to do. Probably anyone younger than age seven may be too young, but try it anyway!)

How to Play:

This is a talking exercise for groups of two or three. Players don't need to "pretend" to be anyone else; they're just basically being themselves: a person having a conversation. The point of the exercise is the talking. The group's job is to make a hypothetical plan for something: it could be what to do after school or on the weekend, it could be planning a party... you should give them a specific situation, so they don't have to take time trying to "think" of something. Once you've explained the exercise, spread the groups around the space and let them all try for a minute or two, all at once.

---

2   *Impro*, pp. 94-100.

As the group tries to make a plan, each person's job is to knock down someone else's suggestion, and then make a new suggestion about what to do (which will in turn be knocked down). This looks something like:

A: Let's go to the park!

B: It's getting too late. Let's go have ice cream.

A: My mom won't let me. Let's have a sleepover.

B: We can't; I don't have a sleeping bag. Let's watch TV.

A: No, there's nothing good on. Let's… climb a mountain.

B: No, I'm scared of heights. Let's… read books.

And so on. It's fun to play with all the different ways to say no:

"Let's go to the zoo!"

"Nope, the zoo's closed."

"We're allergic to animals."

"I hate the zoo!"

There are lots of ways to say no. In many improv circles, that's called **blocking**: cancelling, denying, or invalidating someone else's idea. No matter how elaborate your block — "We can't go to the zoo, because all the animals got together in the middle of the night and staged a dramatic escape and now the police have the city on lockdown and no one is allowed to go anywhere!" — it's still denying the previous person's idea, and therefore it's not constructive.[3] (In a real storytelling situation, if this happened, the next player could remedy the momentary block and build on this idea, saying, "Wow! that sounds amazing! Let's go out and try to track down all the animals!" which definitely sounds like a fun idea

---

3   Of course, these things are fuzzy. Some might argue that by adding all that information, the next player *is* being helpful. Yet, it would be *more* helpful if they began the statement with, "YES, LET'S go to the zoo, because this crazy thing happened and we should help out." A creative denial is still a denial if its primary function is stopping actual story action from going forward.

— but in this exercise, the next person must cancel or deny that situation, and we're still left with absolutely no tower.)

Often, blocking gets a laugh (if there's an audience, which is a great reason to practice it in partners without an audience). But then, there's just nowhere else to go after that. Every new offer has to come from scratch, building from the ground up, and eventually everyone in the group will be frustrated and out of ideas.

Coaching Tips:

After trying the exercise for a minute or two, it's fun to talk about what happened, and even to ask whether any of these things feel familiar from talking to people in real life. They may even be able to come up with a whole slew of other creative ways to say no. Once your group has thought up a variety of different ways to say no, they'll be able to recognize later when someone is employing one of those blocking strategies.

As a side benefit, identifying ways to say no may impact lives more widely than players think. In *Impro*, Keith says, "These 'offer-block-accept' games have a use quite apart from actor training. People with dull lives often think that their lives are dull by chance. In reality everyone chooses more or less what kind of events will happen to them by their conscious patterns of blocking and yielding."[4] If we can identify denial when we hear it from others, we can start to recognize it as it comes out of our own mouths.

---

4   *Impro*, p. 100.

Practice Building the Tower

<u>For: Everyone</u>

How to Play:

The next step is to try planning a trip or event again, using the same framework as the previous exercise and working in partners or small groups — only *this* time, everyone's job is to accept someone's suggestion, and then add something to it.

"Let's go to the zoo!"

"Yeah, and let's bring our sleeping bags!"

"Yeah, and we'll have a sleepover!"

"Yeah, and we'll invite all our friends!"

And so on.

If you're facilitating a big group, it's fun to walk around and listen to these; there's probably going to be a lot of loud voices and possibly jumping up and down. These will probably be crazy adventures that go on and on; they'll probably be dying to tell you about them.

Coaching Tips

As you're walking around listening, make sure that they're not planning an activity where each person does their own unrelated thing; they should at least be in the same universe in these plans. Ideally, it's an adventure that happens to their whole group.

You should also emphasize, in case it isn't clear, that when someone suggests something, that that thing "happens" in their pretend scenario, so that we focus on what comes *next*, and not just listing unconnected things like this:

"Let's eat cake!"

"Yes, and let's go to the moon!"

"Yes, and let's eat lobster!"

"Yes, and let's ride horses!"

If their stories are spinning out of control and widening out sideways, rather than travelling in one narrative line together, you might have them switch to telling the story in the past tense, talking about what they did *already*: "We went to the zoo!" "Yeah, and we saw the lions." "Yeah, and then we climbed into the cages!" "Yeah, and then the lions played with us!" etc. Sometimes pretending it's already happened makes it more clear, especially for younger children, that each action becomes "true" once you say it.

Sometimes when kids — or adults — do this exercise, they get really silly and dark, and their stories involve gross or violent things. That's pretty normal, and it also illustrates the two sides of the same idea: if you're going to embrace that what someone's already said is true, then even gross or violent suggestions become true. The next thing to work on is suggesting things that make sense, and that your compatriots will feel good about accepting. But if they're both having a great time talking about something that grosses you out ... I guess that's just fine.[5]

You probably only need to do this exercise on one occasion, at the beginning of their improv journey, unless they're really really into it. But it's good for building a shared experience to refer to later on, when they're trying other exercises.

---

5   Again, appropriateness boundaries may vary by location.

Practice Messing Up!

<u>For: Everyone</u>

Part of improvising is going to be "messing up." It's just a fact. Most games try to push you to that point of failure and then just past it, so that you can learn from it. So it's very important not to dwell on "failure" in your sessions, and often it's more important to celebrate it. As part of practicing messing up, you can even make up your own silly and joyous "I'm owning failure!" gesture, and have everyone practice it. Patricia Ryan has her students spread their arms wide, grin, and say, "Tadaaaaa!" Laura Derry teaches her students to shoot their arms up in the air and go, "Woohoo!" Whatever it is, it should be big, silly, and happy — definitely not angry or defeated. (You may FEEL bummed out at an actual failure moment, which is all the more reason to own your failure big and loud.)[6] Whatever your fail-moment celebration move is, have everyone learn it and then consciously coach them to use it liberally, no matter what game you're playing.

One game I often play on the first day is what Patricia Ryan used to call the "Circus Bow." Line up the participants and have them, one by one, cycle through the "stage." They must perform a "trick," which, it should be emphasized, must be a really ordinary action, or really barely anything at all. Walking, standing on one leg, waving at someone, shrugging your shoulders… those all count. At the end of the "trick," they

---

6   I don't want to describe Jill Bernard's fabulous game "Loser Ball" because it's hers and it's amazing and it's in HER book … but you should look it up: it's perfect for this purpose.

should plant their feet, face the audience, and bow in a fancy, dignified manner. Everyone watching should applaud wildly.

We do this because we're celebrating every effort. Not every contribution needs to be spectacular in order to count. Often even the absence of obvious "success" is enough to be interpreted as failure. As I repeat constantly to beginning students when we play this game (and in many other contexts), "It doesn't have to be interesting. It just has to be SOMEthing."

As a facilitator, it's important to practice what you preach while teaching this improv stuff. It can be frustrating when things are going wrong or if there are a few kids who are clearly behind the curve in something. It can also be embarrassing if you're the one messing up: if you try something and it doesn't work, if you forget what you're talking about, or if you're modeling an exercise and you "botch" it. But whether you or a student "messed up," it's important to model the same supportive, inclusive behavior. Whenever I'm leading a group of kids, part of my no-stage-fright strategy is to make the kids immediately OK about doing things that seem like "messing up": verbally blanking, getting tagged out in a game, or whatever constitutes a "mistake" in that moment. I usually give them a high five, laugh, and say, "Yes!" or "Nice!" or, "It's OK!" If someone "drops the ball," either literally or figuratively, I help them pick themselves up with jolly good humor, and stop other kids from pointing fingers.

If someone's feeling like they don't want to participate in an exercise, I don't make that an error; I ask them once and then skip them, diverting attention away, which is probably what they want in the moment. What I *don't* do is stop everything and try to reason with them or convince them to do it, while the other kids all egg them on. Even if the other kids intend to be helpful and encouraging, it tends to only makes the problem worse. If a shy student feels like they need to sit slightly apart, or just observe from the circle and not play for a while, I'll let them know it's OK and then I'll divert others' attention away. They'll participate when they feel ready.

More games about SEEING:

What's Different?

<u>For: Everyone</u>

How To Play:

This game works with even very small children (preschool). There are some ways to vary it, but the concept is basically the same. Have the children look around at each other, and then have them close their eyes. You then change one thing; you might tap a child or two and hide them somewhere else in the room, you might have two children switch jackets… and then they all open their eyes, and try to guess what's different. You can also change something about the room if you wish.

Variations:

For older players, you might vary it by having everyone make a tableau, leading *one* person out of the room for a second, and then change something about the tableau. Then the guesser comes back in and tries to find out what's different. In this context, changing something about the people is probably more to the point than changing something about the environment, since we're teaching them to look at and observe each other.

Find the Leader
(Rhythm Maker, Mirror in a circle)

<u>For: Everyone</u>

How to Play:

This is a guessing game, based on observation. My preschool students loved this game, though older children can be more innovative and daring with it. (Generally it's better to be standing, but if the group is scattery or needs a sitting break, you can play this one sitting down too.) One person, the guesser, is sent aside to cover their eyes and ears. Meanwhile, someone in the circle is chosen to be the leader; usually I'll choose, but sometimes I have one of the kids choose. Before we begin I have everyone silently point to the leader to make sure everyone knows who it is. Then the guesser comes back and stands in the middle of the circle, eyes closed. The leader starts making some simple movements, and everyone else mimics them. The followers should all try to mimic the leader's movements in as close to real time as they can — as if they're inside a mirror, making simultaneous movements with the "real person."

When the leading and following is successfully underway, the guesser can open their eyes and start trying to find the leader. They have three guesses. If they guess incorrectly three times, the leader gets to become the guesser in the next round. If the guesser correctly identifies the leader, you can make up what they "win"; I usually let them choose the next guesser.

MANAGED MISCHIEF — GAMES FOR SEEING WHAT'S HAPPENING

Coaching Tips:

Finding the leader relies on observation, because the guesser has to look — and listen — to the people around the circle, in order to identify the leader. For example, as happened just recently in a class of mine, if the leader's first movement is clapping, it'll be pretty easy for the guesser to locate the source of the first clap. And obviously, if everyone's staring directly at the leader, it'll be similarly easy to tell who the leader is, won't it? Eventually the other participants may figure out that if at least SOME people are looking at the leader, everyone else can all look around the circle at each other. The leader, meanwhile, can be coached to make dramatic and sudden changes in movement in order to challenge everyone: go from patting their head, for example, to squatting and patting the floor. This will focus the rest of the players: anyone who isn't quite paying attention and lags a little on the change, well, the guesser can reasonably assume that that person's therefore not the leader. Also, the leader can play with when to change the movements; it's logical to change your movements when the guesser's back is turned, but it's a bold bluff to change when they're looking right at you.

Once you start playing this, EVERYONE will want a turn being the leader. Depending on the size of the group and the time allotted (and the collective attention span), this may or may not be feasible. Once they've gotten the hang of the game, you may choose to divide the group into smaller sub-groups and they can each play, to give more people a chance.

Variations:

Other tricks for exploring the game if you play it for a long time: you might change the challenge or increase the complexity for each round. It might be fun for the group to play around with the guessing aspect of the game. You might see whether leaders can be increasingly sneaky and brave about switching motions while the guesser is looking right at them. You might challenge the rest of the group to find different strategies for following the leader while looking in other directions. You might play a game with the guesser's expectations about who the next leader is going to be, using mischievous misdirection.

You could also give them different physical challenges from round to round. You might challenge the leader to move only their arms, for example, or only their legs. You might suggest that they change levels, moving their whole bodies up high or down low. You might even suggest that they move towards or away from the center of the circle … or even that they dissolve the circle altogether and wander around the room. Why not? Try it! See what happens!

Follow the Follower

For: Age 8 and up

circle; focus; physical

This game is about watching, interpreting, imitating, and following all at once. It's another one for figuring out how to get ideas from someone else, sneakily bypassing one's own internal critic because "someone else thought of it."

How to Play:

This game might also be named, "Let's all do the same thing!" The players start out by standing in the circle, gazing straight ahead but opening their peripheral vision up to catch as many of the other players as possible. They should be standing at "neutral": arms at sides, feet parallel, weight centered over their feet. When the game begins, everyone's job is to gaze at everyone else in the circle and mirror everyone at once with their body. Everyone's job is to watch everyone else, and do what everyone else is doing.

Coaching Tips:

Urge players to look really carefully at everyone else, and copy everything about what's happening. How is everyone standing? Breathing? Are people making sounds? Keep reminding them to look, listen, and mirror.

It's likely that this exercise will move people fairly quickly from neutral posture to a strange tribal ritual. This is normal. The fact that everyone else is looking at everyone else and just trying to mirror them will take the pressure off the individual and put the "weirdness" on the group. The group may indeed collectively end up grunting and pounding on the floor.

If you're doing this exercise and not much is happening, you can urge them to see what everyone else is doing, and just *slightly* exaggerate or mock it. This will hopefully get them to not only mirror but heighten what they see, leading to a giant feedback loop which hopefully will generate some real weirdness.

It's probable that the weirdness will either escalate to the point that it can't get any bigger, or else there will come a moment that feels like the natural ending. Either of those is the perfect time to bring the exercise to a close.

Variations:

You can play a version of this game called "Alien Ritual," and you introduce it by saying that we're visiting another planet where Earth people have never been before, and we must be very polite; they're just about to conduct a very important ritual, and we've been invited to join in. But we don't want to attract attention, we just want to blend in; we better just do what everyone else is doing. That specific direction gives them permission to accept strange movement as normal and possible, because they're expressly trying to blend in with a "non-human" culture. (A lot of theater is just about getting comfortable behaving in ways that fall outside our own personal — and cultural — sense of "normal.")

In practice, this means that everyone stands in a circle, and then you, the leader, can say, "The ritual has begun." At that, the players should all look to each other for physical cues about how this ritual "goes," which means noticing a movement someone else in the circle is making, and joining in. The difference is that in "Follow the Follower," everyone should be following exactly one person, but in "Alien Ritual," players

MANAGED MISCHIEF — GAMES FOR SEEING WH...

should be scanning the whole group, everyone morphing the move at once simultaneously. Again, you can decide when it's over when it seems to have reached a moment that feels like an ending.

...om for the Same Reason

...ish and up

(From Patricia Ryan Madson)

group; audience

This exercise tends to blow people's minds... especially my high school students'. Its most advanced version may be too confusing for littler kids, but for my high schoolers it was a revelation. This exercise had a major impression on me when Patricia Ryan had us do this in our college improv class, and I think it's key to understanding the give and take of offers. This exercise is kind of an onstage-with-other-people-watching exercise, so it needs at least four participants. It's the kind of exercise that's an experiential metaphor: it leads the participants to struggle through and discover for themselves the basic dynamic of working together and accepting each other's ideas in order to move forward. Therefore, explaining it fully to the players ahead of time will probably be both confusing and counterproductive; it's better for *you* to read the explanation, and then lead them through it as I explain below.

It's kind of a weird exercise, and it may feel awkward for people who aren't used to "theater" exercises. Hopefully, reading through the entire explanation will make it seem clearer to you; however, trying it out a few times will be the most illuminating way to explore it. There are just some ways in which theatrical experiences defy verbal description.

How to Play:

Here's the basic scenario: Three people are sitting in chairs, somewhere in a nebulous waiting-room situation. They aren't allowed to talk, and they should be coached away from direct substitutes for verbal communication (mouthing words; playing charades to actively make the other players "guess"). When the exercise begins, their directive is simply this: they all need to leave this imaginary room for the same reason, and once they've hit upon the reason, they should all leave, letting that motivation lead them offstage. Before the first round, that's all the instruction I give. (I tend to do it in three stages or "rounds," with varying augmentation to the instruction, but I don't tell them ahead of time what to "expect" to have happen; I want to see what happens and use everyone's observations to help parse it afterwards. It's important to see what the players do and notice, and also what the "audience" notices. The players' confusion and uncertainty is an important part of what they should experience during this exercise. Just by doing it, they're doing it right.)

Stage One: When you say go (or "lights up!" or "curtain!" or "action!" or whatever your start-the-scene signal is), they should begin their scene: they're sitting there together, existing in the space like real people might in a real waiting room. They could be doing a mimed activity; reading an imaginary newspaper, checking their imaginary watch, or just staring into space. Each may decide, visible through their mimed action, that they have thought of a reason to leave the room (a popular choice is being "late"). They might all be harping away on their own idea. (One person might be furiously looking at their watch and stamping their foot, trying to look "late"; another person might be swatting at bugs, intending to be chased away by insects; the third person might be hiding behind their chair, intending to be "scared.") They might even all rush offstage because of their own idea, disregarding what the others are doing.

If they seem stuck, you can sidecoach, "Find a reason! It needs to be the same reason for every person!" You might hint, "Look at each other!" They might eventually converge on something, having figured out that watching each other is a good idea. The goal is that by looking at each other, they collectively settle upon a single reason for all three of them, and they might do this naturally. But they might not; if they're up there for a minute or two without having exited, you can pause them — then, ask the people watching what they think each person's idea is. Since a large part of this exercise is about teaching genuine observation of the actual present moment, it's a fair bet that the audience, only tasked with observation, will see much more than the people onstage who feel like they have a scary and confusing job to do. Once you've polled the audience, unpause the scene and see if they can agree on something this time.

Don't harp too much on the first group, especially if it was a struggle for them; if they find any sort of reason at all to leave, you can let them rush off in glee. Then call the group back and ask each of them, "What was the reason you left?" They might all have the same answer, or they might have different answers. Either way, it's useful to talk about. They don't have to "get it" completely or talk it to death in order to move on to the next group; letting them puzzle out this exercise is a useful part of the exercise.

You can let the entire group have a chance to try this first round, cycling through all the participants. Each group's experience will be different, depending on the personalities of the people; each group's turn might uncover new questions. If a group gets stuck and can't find a reason to leave, you can remind them, "It doesn't have to be a 'good' reason, it just has to be a reason." Have to leave the because they're all sneezing too much? That's a perfectly fine reason; it doesn't need to make Logical Sense. Or, players might be having a good time coming up with more and more complicated ideas, which you can see they've pre-planned while they were sitting. Each time a group leaves, ask them after the scene, "What was your reason for leaving?" If the idea was one particular person's complicated idea, they might be the one explaining it, while the others will probably seem cheerful but surprised that the idea contained so many specific details. This is a signal that they're learning to go along, but that the "idea-haver" is getting too complex and not conveying everything that they're thinking.

Stage Two: When they seem like they've gotten the point so far, tell them, "This time, don't 'think of an idea.' Don't try to do anything. Watch each other, and be inspired by what someone else is doing." If they're paying attention, someone might then ask the logical question, "But, if we're not supposed to do anything… huh?" "You'll see," I usually say. Again, put them on three chairs in a nebulous room, and tell them to go. If they're confused, you might want to sidecoach them, "Look at each other."

If they're having problems, you can freeze the scene and ask the audience, "What are they doing right now? What's 'happening?'" The audience may have a lot to describe. The sneaky thing is, the group onstage is probably not sitting completely at neutral, and anything they might be doing, consciously or unconsciously, can inspire a scene partner to pick up on it. Someone might accidentally scratch their leg, or push their hair back, or sneeze — or they might just be looking absently at a particular place in space. The audience will notice everything that's happening, down to the players' facial expressions. The "thing" is just whatever someone happens to notice and copy. See what's happening … help it happen. Again, it doesn't have to be "good" or "the best thing," it just has to be something that happens twice. In seeing and repeating "pushing my hair back," they may not even know quite what they mean by the gesture. But by copying and amplifying it, they're reinforcing its importance; the players can discover what it means. Hopefully, all three of them pick up on it, and start amplifying it, and it escalates enough to take them offstage.

Let everyone try the second round version, seeing if you can really get them to look at each other and only use "each other's" ideas... if they can do it, it may completely reshape their universe. This is also a sharing-control exercise, because it forces children to drop their own idea in favor of someone else's idea (even if the "idea" is something that someone else made you think of). It teaches openness to a situation, in lieu of bringing your own preformed plan and making everyone else conform to it.

Coaching Tips:

If the players are confused about what they can be doing physically, you can tell them it's OK to mime actions, but not in order to play "charades." The difference is that charades is a guessing game, wherein nothing can continue until the players correctly guess the exact thing that the mime was trying to convey. In that scenario, one player is forcibly thrusting their idea onto everyone else, not accepting any alternatives. The idea with this exercise, on the other hand, is that each player displays their own behavior while observing the behavior of others. Everyone is responsible for paying attention to each other; no one's held hostage by having to correctly identify someone else's idea before moving forward. It's more like real life; the observation and the conclusions are a constant give-and-take. The person who originates a gesture has made an offer, but the other players' interpretation of that gesture has equal weight to the "original idea."

I think this exercise is extremely valuable, since it lets you learn to enter into a situation with a completely blank slate, secure in the notion that all you have to do is look to someone else for inspiration and an idea will come.

This exercise was also fundamental in building that seventeen-person high school ensemble, since I told them, in order to do a scene with seventeen people onstage, they just needed to find the very first thing, and go with that. The first thing that "happens" is what they're going to build the scene on. It becomes the base of the tower that you're all going to build together. I recently led this exercise with a group of adults: a beginning improv class at a theater. They were puzzled at first, and then in processing the exercise afterward, they asked the important fundamental questions, about what makes a scene work: "So am I supposed to keep my idea, or go with someone else's idea?" The answer is, a little of both: if you see someone else's idea, you don't need to throw your idea away quite yet (hold on tightly). As long as your idea and their idea can exist at the same time, you can try to keep both going on. But if the tide is going in a direction that's making your original idea less and less relevant, it's okay to "let go lightly," and follow along with the group plan. In their specific class, during the first round of this game someone was pretending to be ill, a second person was helping her, and the third person was sitting in disgust off to one side, trying not to catch the disease. It's a valid choice to act disgusted here, but by just sitting and being disgusted without *also* contributing to the group activity, *no one's* meeting the objective of the scene, which is for the group of three to leave together for the same reason. The third character eventually overcame her disgust and got up to help out, and the three of them successfully left the room.

I recently played this with another group of adults, a more experienced group of improvisors, and the "thing" that happened was that they all started stomping and clapping and becoming a band … but then they stopped. It petered out after about a minute, and they all sat there looking defeated. I paused them and said, "It seems like you found the thing already; keep doing it, and let it take you offstage!" They said, "Well, that didn't seem like it would get us to leave the room," and I said, "It doesn't have to make logical 'sense'; you've found the thing, and now it just has to carry you out of the room, so let it get big enough to do that." They tried again, and this time they all became so transported by their clapping and stomping that they had to stand up and dance and bang on the chairs, and they all danced offstage with wild abandon. "That's it!" I said.

They had figured out that simply choosing one "thing" to work on together, and making that thing as big and important as possible, was enough to make the scene work. Sometimes we think that what we're doing isn't "enough," so instead of following through, we look around for other things to do also, or instead, and we all slowly lose steam because we gave up too early. Or, we back off because we feel that exploring the first thing might get us into uncomfortable territory: did dancing offstage feel too "silly" for these grownups? It's easier to simply focus on what that first "thing" is, and fully explore its different aspects: how does it make us feel? How can we magnify that activity or take it to the next level? What might happen next logically, as a result of what's happened so far? By going to extremes with what might have seemed at first to be a strange and arbitrary choice, we can find the new, the absurd, and the delightful.

GAMES FOR HELPING IT HAPPEN

Being Constructive, One Thing at a Time

This category of games is about practicing being directly, immediately constructive. If we're not working together, it's immediately obvious.

One-something-at-a-time

<u>For: Everyone</u>

group; circle; pairs; multimedia

One-thing-at-a-time is a fun way to collaborate. Each person adds a piece, so that the finished thing is truly a product of the whole group. There are lots and lots of ways to make things in this fashion—anything you can conceive of that is constructed with separate elements. You could add words together to make sentences, rules, letters, poems, stories, etc. You could add letters together to make words. You could also add notes to make songs, moves to make dances, lines to make drawings, and so on.. The following pages list some of the many exercises you could try.

Word-at-a-time (Sentences or Rules)

How to Play:

Standing in a circle (or in partners), the group creates individual sentences, with each person adding one word at a time. The goal is to make sentences that make sense, and not to throw in words that are crazy on purpose and make no sense syntactically. This game can be tough for beginners, so it's a good idea to start with single sentences that don't have to be connected to one another; a successful sentence makes everyone feel successful. It's fun to do word-at-a-time Wise Sayings, which are general rules for living (or rules for the classroom); if they're rules, it can also help people who freeze up at the idea of thinking of the first word of a sentence by suggesting to start a rule with "Always" or "never." It's OK for the sentences to be silly (ie, not "real" rules for the classroom) as long as they make grammatical sense. You don't want "Always try to REFRIGERATOR!" but "Always try to put your socks in the refrigerator!" is OK.

How to figure out where the end of the sentence is? A sentence is complete when it "feels" over. The person whose turn it is decides whether the sentence is over: if they add another word, the sentence is still going, but if they choose not to, then the sentence is finished! I like to have the group repeat the sentence, all together, and then add a little wise bow, muttering "Yesyesyesyesyes" while patting fingertips together in a pseudo-prayer position. It helps reinforce the validity and wisdom of the sentence that was just created — especially if that sentence was quite silly. When a sentence is finished, create another one, and keep going until you find a good place to stop.

Coaching Tips:

Gently urge players not to think too much; the game goes best when it goes fast. It doesn't have to be the "best" word; just the first word that comes to you that makes sense.

When they start playing this game, kids are usually DYING to put words in the mouths of others; if someone is stumped for a few seconds, there will probably be other kids squirming and calling out the word they think should come next. Especially if you've thought of a completely brilliant sentence, how agonizing is it to have someone say something else instead? Arrrgh! Make sure to remind them whose turn it is; everyone gets to add a word when it's *their turn*. When it's your turn, you alone get to decide what word to add. It's an important lesson of "word-at-a-time" that your "obvious" is not the same as other people's, and that it's OK to let your plan go, in favor of someone else's idea. That's another good reason to repeat the sentence once it's completed: not only does it reinforce listening and memory, but it slyly reinforces that, even if everyone had their own sentence in mind, the sentence that was actually created as a group was still weird and wonderful.

Groups do improve at this game; if your group is getting the hang of it, you could try letting the sentences gradually relate to each other in some way. (The group might even start doing this by themselves; humans are always on the lookout for making connections between things.) If the group is excited about making chains of sentences that might be approximating a narrative, they're probably ready for **Word-at-a-time Story** (below).

MANDY KHOSHNEVISAN

Word-at-a-Time Character/Expert

For: Age 7 and up

audience

HOW TO PLAY:

Another fun way to play word-at-a-time is to have a group of people play one character, who happens to speak one word at a time. (Usually it's two or three people, but it could be as many as you like!) Someone could interview that character, like in a talk-show type interview. Maybe the word-at-a-time character is just an ordinary person you'd like to know more about, or maybe they're a famous expert on something. Perhaps they're simply an oracle or advice columnist, and the interviewer is just seeking advice on a variety of topics. Like in any interview, you can start with simple questions like "What's your name?" and gradually build up to finding out more about their point of view on all manner of subjects. Feel free to ask them questions about basically anything, especially if it involves their opinion on something that the players themselves probably know nothing about. An interview is a particularly rewarding format to practice word-at-a-time, since answers are typically one sentence long, which is simple to achieve, and it's probably not going to be a "right" answer, which means it'll be deliciously silly.

You might also interact with a many-headed character in a scene, by creating a situation with two characters in it — one of whom happens to be a word-at-a-time character. Or in a more advanced version, have two word-at-a-time characters talk to each other; maybe they're on a date, or having a job interview, or who knows what? You could determine their relationship before starting the scene, or the players could discover their relationship in conversation.

Coaching Tips:

The convention in this game is to refer to word-at-a-time characters using singular pronouns, intimating that they're one person, not multiple people. "He," "she" and "I," not "we" and "they." Also, the more excited and happy the interviewer (or other character) is to talk to the word-at-a-time character, the more fun everyone will have. The interview process will be most successful and rewarding if the interviewer takes every opportunity to repeat the word-at-a-time answers, and acts awed and impressed by the interviewee's wisdom and insight.

Word-at-a-time Story

<u>For: Everyone, but might be easier with ages 8 and up.</u>

group; circle; partners

How to Play:

The next step after word-at-a-time sentences is word-at-a-time stories, going around the circle (or back and forth between partners) adding one word at a time, telling a story together as a single narrator.

Coaching Tips:

Keeping a word-at-a-time story on track can be more difficult (even for very experienced improvisors), so make sure to celebrate success and cheerfully avoid dwelling on failures.

These stories don't have to be long. They can be very short. They may very well be weird and inscrutable. We can examine the meaning of a word-at-a-time story when the story is over, for it may be unfathomable and abstract. It may be weird. But weird abstractness can still be delightful and feel very meaningful. I recommend trying a few after giving just the bare minimum of instructions, to "see what happens" — what this particular group tends to produce.

These stories go off track in some predictable patterns: They might have the hero die right away. There might not even be a hero at all; it might be about a non-active inanimate object, or a group of people, or something else that proves not to be great at making decisions or creating action. The focus might keep switching, resulting in a sequence of largely

MANAGED MISCHIEF — GAMES FOR HELPING IT HAPPEN

unconnected sentences. There might be a sequence of events that goes on and on and on and on and on and on. In these cases, you might suggest rudimentary story-structure ideas like, "Why don't we try having the next one be about a main character?" or, "Why don't we see what it's like to try having a beginning, middle, and end?" The discovery process is as important as the successful-storytelling process sometimes, so don't push TOO hard with "advice" unless the exercise is a part of a specific session focusing on story structure. Sometimes, talking about what happened in a particular story will be enough to lead participants to *discover* story structure, and a discovery is more valuable than an instruction, in many cases. It's OK to let things stew and come back to the game another time. (You may also choose to make use of the Story Spine when teaching this exercise.)

It's also perfectly OK to stop a story that seems to be crashing and burning and spiraling out of control. In case of story-emergency, Keith Johnstone recommends the group gleefully shout, "AGAIN!" and then beginning a new story. It's a great opportunity to demonstrate yet again the cheerful acknowledgment of — and rebound from — "failure."

You might set a time limit and arbitrarily declare a certain place to be the end. To give it some closure, you might say, "Let's say the moral of the story, one word at a time!" Then create the moral of the story that you just told (no matter whether it ended satisfyingly or not). You may well surprise yourself how uncannily insightful it turns out to be, or how much unexpected meaning the moral may lend to a story that just seemed weird, before.

Splitting up into pairs to create quick word-at-a-time stories is one of my favorite improv warmups for a show or workshop, since it gets players connecting, making eye contact, and working one-on-one together without an audience or anyone else watching.

Word-at-a-time Writing

<u>For: Ages 7 and up</u>

group, partners, circle; quiet time; writing

HOW TO PLAY:

You can also play word-at-a-time games in writing, passing a paper around and each player adding one word. In the beginning, this works best if the piece of writing has a predetermined format: writing a letter is a fun choice, but it could also be a diary entry, a ransom note, or whatever you like. Writing a story works too, but somehow everyone writing together in the first-person voice, as in a letter, makes the end result feel more delightful.

Coaching Tips:

In any word-at-a-time writing, it's good to remind writers to read the whole thing so far, before adding the next word. It's probably also worth reminding them that the word that comes next should be the word that seems obvious. (The magic lies in the fact that, again, something that seems obvious to one person is entirely miraculous to another. It's all right to trust your "obvious" choice.)

Line-at-a-time Poem

For: Ages 7 and up

group, partners, circle; quiet time; writing

HOW TO PLAY:

Determine a structure for the poem, if you like (haiku? limerick? sonnet? another kind of poem with a specific rhyme scheme?), and then write it, one line at a time. You could structure this as a public group process, where one person writes it on a paper or on the board while people verbally add lines one at a time. You could do this as a quiet activity, passing papers around the room. You could pass the poem through every person, or you could do it in partners. Everyone could start with their own paper, writing their own first line and then either trading with one partner or passing all the poems on, say, around in a circle.

MANDY KHOSHNEVISAN

Thing-at-a-time Drawing

For: Everyone

art, quiet time

How to Play:

Something-at-a-time even works as a drawing game, with each participant adding one "thing" each time. Again, giving it a specific format or structure will help direct the piece to a unified result; for example, a good way to introduce the exercise is as a portrait, starting with two dots on the page to represent where the eyes go.[1] You could try it with it another format: landscape, still life, map, etc. When you're done drawing, it's also fun to title your picture or name the portrait subject, adding one letter at a time. (How fun would it be to draw a map and then name things one letter at a time?! You could be at it all day!) This would be a great activity for, say, waiting around anywhere you might have a piece of paper and something to write with (or a smartphone/tablet and your finger).

---

1   I think this is from Keith Johnstone?

Note-at-a-Time Chord

<u>For: Everyone</u>

music, circle, group

I love this simple activity: it builds familiarity with singing-type sounds, especially harmony-type singing, and it always sounds interesting.

HOW TO PLAY:

Everyone stands in a circle; one person sings (and holds) a note with a particular vocal quality on a specific vowel. Travelling around the circle, each person adds and holds their own note, trying to match the first person's vowel and vocal quality, but singing whatever note comes out of their mouth. As each person adds their note, they should hold it steady, taking breaths as needed but keeping the same note, as everyone adds in to join them, so that by the end, everyone is holding a note at once. (You can designate that each chord is a specific number of people, like four, or you can have the whole circle contribute to every chord.) When everyone in the chord has added their note, the first person uses their hands (or other body parts, as inspired?) to conduct the "cutoff," the moment when everyone stops singing.

Variations:

The leader of the chord can experiment with different ways to direct the cutoff, so that everyone stops successfully at once, as intended. The group can talk about it: what kinds of movements might work better than others? What have we observed so far that's worked? The chord leader can also use gestures to conduct the chord itself while it's still going, seeing if they can coach the group to get louder, softer, or change their sound or pitch in some way (scoop upwards? fall downward? pulse? what else might be fun?). Again, once they've discovered these variations, the group can talk about what gestures work better and for which purposes.

Rather than a single note, the person who starts the chord might experiment with a sound that moves somehow: a chant, perhaps, or a sentence, or an animal sound, or something else that seems fun.

Coaching Tips:

The Merriam-Webster Online Dictionary defines "chord" simply as: "three or more musical tones sounded simultaneously." Very important: when playing this game, there are NO WRONG NOTES. The note that comes out of your mouth first is the CORRECT NOTE. No matter how much singing experience you have or don't have, you can physically make a musical tone with your voice, and the one you make is, again, the CORRECT NOTE. Your note may be higher than the person's before you, or it may be lower. It may even be the same! It may not even be the note you thought you were going to sing. Regardless, sing it loud and proud, without trying to sneak it to another note. Per my definition, if people are singing the same note, it's unison. If they're not, it's harmony. Either way, it counts as a chord.

People may laugh or cringe if a particular chord sounds "terrible," but feel free to point out that plenty of fancy musicians write all kinds of unusual harmonies in Real Music, and that dissonance often sounds really cool! Some chords that you create might be beautiful, and some might be dissonant, strange, or haunting, but any chord is interesting and fun to explore. And one person's note does not "ruin" a chord; building a chord with the group means agreeing to accept all the notes that get added.

Training one's ear to find notes that might be conventionally harmonious with other notes is certainly a skill which can be improved upon, and if your group is interested in working on that some more, you might try examining more closely what kinds of notes sound more harmonious. You don't need to stop and start, but you could talk about what kinds of notes sound more like conventional harmonies, and which ones sound more dissonant. You could have the whole group hold the same note, while each person takes a turn moving their voice against the single note, experimenting with high and low notes, close to and farther away from the held note, just discovering what it sounds like. Keep in mind that it's all in the name of experimentation and exploration, regarding people's singing choices as *choices* to be examined, rather than mistakes to be corrected.

Thing-at-a-time Soundscape

For: Everyone

music, circle, sounds

How to Play:

Standing in a circle, one person starts a rhythmic and repeated musical phrase, using their voice. Each person, traveling around the circle, adds their own repeated sound or phrase. When everyone has added their voice, the one who started the soundscape can conduct the group if they wish, changing the volume or other qualities of the soundscape; the conductor (the person who started the soundscape) might even raise or lower the volume of specific people. The conductor can lead the piece to an end, or else they might see if the group can find a natural ending together.

Coaching Tips:

Making musical-type sounds with one's voice can be very scary (this is even more true the older we get). Encourage players to make actual vocalizations, rather than just pushing air through (like a "shhhhhh" or a "ch-ch-ch-ch" sound). If it helps make people more focused or more comfortable, you could ask players to close their eyes.

See if the players can keep to a repeatable sound, that also keeps in the same rhythm with others' sounds; that way if the conductor is trying to get the whole group to speed up or slow down, it will be clear what's happening and also how everyone's part still fits with the other parts in the new tempo. The soundscape can be abstract, but players will hopefully "help it happen" by responding to something that they observe, either by matching someone else, or providing a complement or direct opposite to something they've noticed. For example, if there are lots of beep-boop noises already happening, a player might think, "Maybe we're robots!" and make some similar sounds. Or, a player might want to provide a bed for these beep-boop noises by singing a low, consistent drone. You can talk about players' choices after the soundscape is over, if you wish, but once again, don't try to overexplain it beforehand.

Variations:

Rather than starting from scratch, you can choose an inspiration for the piece: a word? a style of music? a feeling? and create a sound picture of that specific concept.

For a different, more literal kind of soundscape, you could choose a location and go around the circle each adding vocal sound effects to create the radio-play ambiance of that location: for example, a restaurant might have murmuring customers, slurping sounds, background music, clinking dishes, people in the kitchen, etc. See if you can find musical rhythms while imitating everyday sounds… this soundscape can also be conducted to change the volume or the tempo, and to find its ending.

Soloing: You can create a soundscape that functions like a jazz song, where everyone takes turns soloing while still supported by the other players in the background. Establish a soundscape as usual, with every person in turn adding a repetitive musical phrase until the whole circle is playing. Then, take turns doing solos: either travel around the circle, or else have the conductor indicate who should solo next. The soloist should get louder, and everyone else should get a little softer (but keep playing). The soloist can begin by simply making their own rhythmic piece louder;

then, they can vary different aspects of it, exploring the sounds they're already making. If I'm imitating a drum sound, for example, during my solo I might repeat my rhythmic phrase a few times as I'd established it, and then I might see if I can play it really fast, or really slow, or make some parts of it really loud and others very soft; I might take that opportunity to see what other sounds I can make that sound like a drum. I can decide to end my solo myself, by returning to my usual phrase, or the conductor can decide by gesturing for someone else to solo, instead.

Instruments: You can create a soundscape nonverbally, focusing more on the interactions of rhythms. You might have players create their rhythm using body percussion, clapping, stomping or snapping different rhythms. You might use found objects or homemade instruments: chairs, spoons, pencils, rulers… what else around you makes a noise? You might even use "real" musical instruments — or any combination of the above: physical percussion, found objects, musical instruments, *and* voices. With instruments, you can try all the variations: creating a themed soundscape, creating a sound-picture of a location, and taking turns with soloing.

Orchestra: If inspired, you can even arrange players into "sections" as in an orchestra, all facing the conductor. You can create sections based on whatever concept seems the most fun and the most appropriate to your group and your activity. You may decide to let the current conductor subdivide the orchestra according to their inspiration. There might be a "voices" section, an "instruments" section, a "brass" section, an "animal noises" section … Or you might have an "emotional" orchestra, and have sections representing different emotions. Colors, seasons, books, periods in history… what are you inspired by? Use your imagination and try things out!

MAKING OFFERS WITH YOUR VOICE

Sometimes just speaking out loud can be a breakthrough, never mind speaking persuasively or decisively. This category of games helps players practice making bold, confident offers using their voices, either verbally or very non-verbally.

Note-at-a-time Chord

(page 119)

Soundscape

(page 122)

Sound Ball

(page 155)

Counting to 10 Together

<u>For: Everyone</u>

circle, focus, give and take; group mind.

This is a good centering exercise to teach give-and-take.

How to Play:

Stand in a circle, ideally with eyes closed, though you could play it with eyes open. The starting goal is to count to ten as a group, one person at a time. The catch is, only one person can talk at a time; if two voices overlap, you have to start over from one. The idea is not to figure out how to beat the system by "planning," going in order around the circle, for instance; the idea is to develop the idea of group mind, filling in when needed, and taking turns.

Coaching Tips:

At the beginning, it's often slow going, and can be frustrating, especially if they have to keep resetting to one. If the players get frustrated, have everyone take a deep breath and shake out physically; usually, the more anxious you get about trying to "win" this game, the harder it becomes. You'll get there… and if you don't, you can set a smaller goal: eight? five? Whatever the group's personal best becomes, it can be lauded as a record. The goal is to improve with time.

Variations:

Once everyone's got the hang of it, you can move to the next level and try counting to 20, or see if you can say the alphabet. If that becomes an easy task and the players are still interested, you can try to see how high you can count.

Alphabet Lists!

<u>For: Everyone who can name words starting with specific letters of the alphabet</u>

pairs, circle, group, rapid fire

How to Play:

Pick a category of something, and then go through the alphabet in sequence, taking turns letter by letter, naming things in that category. During warmups for shows, when we have to exercise our "naming muscle," we often do "first names" or "last names," but you could also do fruits, vegetables, countries, cities, animals, or any other category you can think of. For example, fruits:

"Apple!"

"Banana!"

"Canteloupe!"

"Durian!"

"Eggplant!"

The "rule" of the alphabet gives you some structure, so you don't have to think of something "from nothing." You should go quickly, and say the first thing that comes to your head. Clearly some letters will be easier than others, so go ahead and say the first thing you think of. Your first thought may be weird and make you laugh, and if so, you're on the right track. And "cheating" doesn't really mean anything in this game. Is "eggplant" a fruit? Maybe! It was the first thing I thought of. If "Xtra Big Apple" is the only fruit beginning with X that comes to mind, say that!

You're already winning. (I've been known to play this game just driving around in the car with my roommate. Because it's fun.)

Three Things!

<u>For: Everyone</u>

pairs, circle, rapid-fire

A firing-line kind of warmup game, to get the synapses firing.

How to Play:

Someone turns to their neighbor and says, "Three things that _____" It might be: Three things that are blue? Three things that are tall? Three things that are fast? The neighbor lists three things, and the whole group shouts, "Three things!" The person who just named three things turns to *their* neighbor, and says, "Three things that _____!" and the game continues around the circle.

The idea is to name the first three things that come to your mind, whether or not they're "right" (that is, whether or not they strictly fulfill the terms of the challenge), and whether or not they make a lot of sense. For example:

"Three things that are blue!"

"Blueberries, blue socks, blue cereal!"

Speed is preferred over "accuracy." Also, try to train players away from, "Uhhhhhhhh………." Often what happens is people will think they're sneakily filling the need to speak right away by saying a filler word, but then they'll just hang out in it while they're thinking:

"Three things that start with the letter L!"

"Uhhhhhhhhhhhhhhhhhhhhhhhhhhhhhhhhhhhhh lemons! Uhhhhhhhhhhhhhhhh…."

MANAGED MISCHIEF — MAKING OFFERS WITH

Et cetera. (By the way, people who use these filler wo_ pulling status, by reserving the available air so that no one els_ even if they themselves haven't thought of a thing to say yet.) Al_ confidence in merely uttering a sound, we want to encourage confi_ _e in saying a specific word, without apologizing for it by prefacing it with "uhhhh." One way to practice what it feels like to say a word right away is, instead of using an empty filler word like "uhhhhh," is to just start vocalizing a letter or syllable, and your brain will complete the word for you *as* it's emerging from your mouth:

"Three things that are green!"

"Fffffffoliage!"

Coaching Tips:

To answer a possible question that might be in your mind: does anyone have to remember or repeat these three things? Does anyone ever have to say them ever again? Nope! The exercise is just in coming up with three things, as quickly as possible.

Variations:

"Seven Things": I bet you can guess why it's called that.

"Popcorn"-style: Instead of travelling around the circle, you might have players send it to specific people by calling their name. "Laura!" "Yeah?" "Three things that are old!"

To reinforce "right answers," you might have the group shout, "Yes!" after every answer, or else they might count, "One!" "Two!" "Three!" after every answer until they get to "Three Things!" (or, "Seven Things!")

"Things Three": One of my improv groups, possibly the Stanford Improvisors, made up the opposite exercise, "Things Three," where the person gives a list of three things, and the response is to categorize them: "Fish, Cow, Cat!" "Three things I have as pets." And then the group repeats, "Things three!"

GAMES FOR CIRCLES 10

It's fun to stand in a circle! Like King Arthur's fabled Round Table: it's very egalitarian. You can see everyone, no one can hide behind anyone else, and also no one feels like they're completely onstage. It's like everyone's in the audience and onstage at the same time, which is great for building community.

Some of these circle games are like "warmups"... improvising together involves a whole variety of mental skills, and just like real muscles, your little brain-muscles get stronger the more you practice them. Listening, memory, following a structure while coming up with ideas that fit into the structure... all of these are skills we use when working together. A circle is the easiest and most democratic form to practice these skills.

Circle games are all suited for structured group improv time, and all of them are fun in different ways. Your group of people may be delighted by a certain kind of game more than others, depending on the specific alchemy of personalities: some groups are more delighted by wordplay, some prefer big physical games, some like making music and sounds... There's value in occasionally practicing the skills that may be more difficult for some groups, to work those mental muscles; there's also value in following the group's happiness and playing games that they really like. The more invested a group is in a certain activity, the more they have the potential to find "the game of the game" and evolve it into something new and more complex, that may become their "own game."

MANDY KHOSHNEVISAN

Word-at-a-time rules or stories
(page 110)

One thing-at-a-time anything
(page 109)

Find the Leader
(Rhythm Maker, Mirror in a Circle)
(page 96)

Yes (or Go)

<u>For: Everyone</u>

circle, attention, focus, eye contact

This warmup is about seeing each other, and being present and ready to move.

How to Play:

Stand in a circle. Everyone's feet are glued to the floor. Point at someone. They say "Yes," and you start walking towards them to take their spot. Right away, they point at someone else; when they hear a "yes," they start moving to that person's spot. Repeat.

Variations:

You can say "Go" instead of "yes" if you want to; that emphasizes the speed goal, to get someone else to tell you "go" before the person gets to your spot.

You may morph this into a name-game exercise: when someone points at you, instead of saying "yes" or "go," say the pointer's name. (Or you could build it into two phases; in Phase 1, you say your own name when someone points at you, and in Phase 2, you can say *their* name.)

To make it sillier, see if the players can notice, imitate, and amplify the *way* in which others are saying "go" or "yes," or the way that they're walking across the circle, so that the simple neutral action becomes bigger and more specific. (For example, if someone's taking teeny tiny steps in order to give the next person more time, that person might say "Go!" in a teeny tiny voice and travel using even smaller steps, and the next person might notice and amplify *that*, and so on.)

To make the exercise more about subtlety, use a solid eye contact instead of pointing. To make it even subtler, replace the spoken "yes" with just a nod, so the game is entirely silent.

Circle Pattern Games

There are lots of variations of these circle-game pattern warmups. Here are two basic umbrella structures for pattern games; each way works a different mental muscle. In "You" (or variations thereof), every person contributes just one step in the pattern, but the complexity comes in layering several patterns at once, so players must learn to deal with and sort multiple inputs at the same time. In "Word Bridges," the group works together to make one long pattern that snakes back and forth between players several times; the complexity comes in making the pattern longer, and switching the direction of travel forward and backward, so players must remember the same information from multiple angles.

You (or "Circuits")

For: Ages 4 and up

Pattern, attention/focus, eye contact, memory; filtering information through chaos

HOW TO PLAY:

Easy procedures for forming a pattern: I've learned two possible ways to indicate this physically. Method number one: Have everyone put their right hand up and point to the ceiling. The person who starts the pattern brings their hand down to point at a specific person. That person swings their hand down to point at someone else, and so on until no hands point at the ceiling; the last person should send the pattern back to the start. Method number two: The first person puts one hand on their head and points the other at someone else in the circle. That person puts their own hand on their head to show they've been chosen, and sends the pattern to someone else; repeat through everyone, and the last person should point to the first person again. You can of course use either method, or make up your own. I happen to like hands on heads; it's sillier.

First pattern: Using the procedure you like best, the first person begins the pattern by pointing to someone else and saying "You." That person points at someone else and says "You." The chain goes through everyone and then back to the first person. Hands down and no more pointing, repeat that same exact pattern of "You"s again, so that the pattern returns again to the first person; one circuit completed. You can practice that a few times to make sure everyone's got it.

Adding a second pattern: Setting the first pattern metaphorically aside, the first person/leader can create a new pattern with another set of words, usually in a specific category (Colors! Emotions! Animals!) to keep track of which pattern is which. Create the second pattern the same way as the first: the leader sends their word to someone, the next person sends it to someone else, and so on until everyone in the circle is included in the pattern exactly once. (Encouraging players to point at a different person in the second pattern will make things easier later.) Practice repeating this new pattern a few times. Now, review the first pattern, the "You" pattern.

Now, try to do both patterns at once! The leader starts the "You" pattern going around a few times, sending it on again when it comes back to the beginning. Once that's established, and traveling round and round the circle, send out the second pattern too, and try to keep THAT going — at the same time!

When you're feeling confident, stop all the patterns for a moment, and create a third pattern in a different category. Now, start the first one, and then the second one, and then the third one, and try to keep them all going round and round at the same time. You can do it! You're amazing! Feeling more amazing? Add more patterns!

The key is: each person is responsible for a successful handoff of the pattern to the next person. When there's more than one thing going on, it's hard for people to be looking and listening everywhere at once. Therefore, if you can see they didn't hear you the first time, say it again: use your eye contact and your voice to send it multiple times, if necessary, and make sure they got it. It's also entirely possible that one person might receive both patterns at once; if that happens, they don't need to panic; they can just send first one, and then the other.

Variations for Young Children:

To make this more concrete for small people, you can create a pattern using an actual object, like a small ball or beanbag.[1] To start this pattern, say someone's name and then toss them the object. They should, in turn, say someone else's name and toss the object. Everyone should receive the object exactly once, and the first person to toss the object is the last person to receive it, so that the pattern goes in one complete circuit. (It's a good idea to play this version while saying names out loud; it's a good attention-getting device, hopefully preventing anyone from getting a beanbag to the face.)

For very small children, one circuit might be plenty to accomplish; with a group that has conquered the single-object version, you could add additional patterns using objects that are physically different from each other, so that players can tell the difference between patterns.

Advanced Variations:

For listening and building word connections: Rather than decide the category ahead of time, see if the group can build the category based on what's already in the category (like verbal "I am a Tree"). The first person, thinking, Pets? might say "Dog," for example; the next person might say "Elephant" and now the category seems like Animals. (The third person might see something different and say "Table," clearly thinking "Things With Four Legs." You never know.)

Super-Advanced Version:

We used to do a crazy version using only each other's names:

---

[1] Why oh why are Koosh balls so hard to find nowadays? Those work perfectly for this game. My preschoolers in the 2015 school year were absolutely transfixed by my sole remaining Koosh ball.

The first pattern, you say the name of the person you're pointing at (instead of "You").

The second pattern, you say your own name.

The third pattern, you say the name of the person who gave you the pattern (to start it, the first person picks someone to point at them, and then sends that person's name to someone else).

Un-Scripted got so good at this game that we eventually added a fourth pattern: you say the name of the person that they should send the pattern to next.

Coaching Tips:

Any variation of this multiple-pattern game is really useful for focus and filtering; it teaches your brain how to zone in on the important information amidst a lot of unrelated chaos. (I like to think that it trains a skill that gets underdeveloped thanks to internet multitasking: how to focus amidst a multimedia barrage of sensory information.) The first one or two times you might try this game with young students, they may get confused, frustrated, and bored. Patterns will get lost. Kids will talk and laugh. The first few times, it's good to play up success and downplay "doing-it-wrong." If it's really hard, celebrate whenever a pattern successfully completes a circuit and makes it back to you. (I usually let them go around a few times and then "catch" them as they come back to me, so there's a successful endpoint.) You can present it as a challenge: "Maybe next week we can do two patterns at a time, or three." After playing it a few times on a few different occasions, they tend to figure it out, and it becomes a good centering exercise.

Word Bridges

(or, The Word-Association Pattern Game)

<u>For: Age 9 and up</u>
Pattern, focus; memory; patterns; listening

This is a more advanced version of the previous game. I learned it from people at Curious Comedy in Portland, OR; I'm not sure where the exercise comes from originally. This exercise is great for learning to listen and to remember words that you've said and also that someone else has said. In its advanced stage, it is one long pattern that continues through several rounds, wandering its way to everyone in the circle several times so that everyone's got several words to say. It helps if players take care to send words to different people in each round; it makes it easier to remember.

How to Play:

This game is tricky to explain and slightly simpler to demonstrate, but here I shall try. Someone starts the pattern by sending a word to someone across the circle. That person continues the pattern by passing a word that they free-associate with the first word:

    A to B: Paper
    B to C: Write
    C to D: Wrong
    D to E: Choice
    E to F: Chopper

F to G: Helicopter
G to A: Airplane
A to C: Fly
... etc.

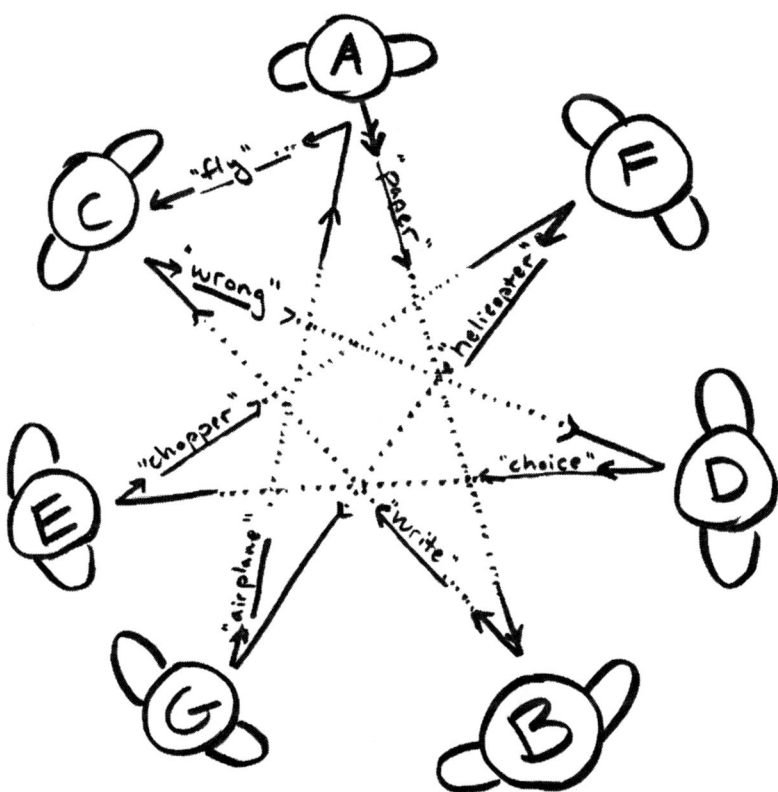

(That's what it looks like visualized.)

(Players shouldn't repeat words that others have already said — it will make the game Too Confusing.) The first time you play this game, you might want to complete just one circuit, so that everyone has one word and the pattern returns to the leader. For more advanced players, you can create a longer pattern that bounces around through everyone a few times before coming to stop at the leader.

When the leader determines that the pattern is finished, restart the pattern and run through it a few times, keeping it exactly the same each time. Help players remember, if they forget what comes next, until everyone has the pattern down.

Now, picture this pattern as a series of bridges between people, and each bridge has a word painted on it. To cross the bridge in either direction, say the word painted on the bridge. In the example given above, B gives "Write" to C, but C can also give "Write" back to B by crossing the same bridge in the other direction.

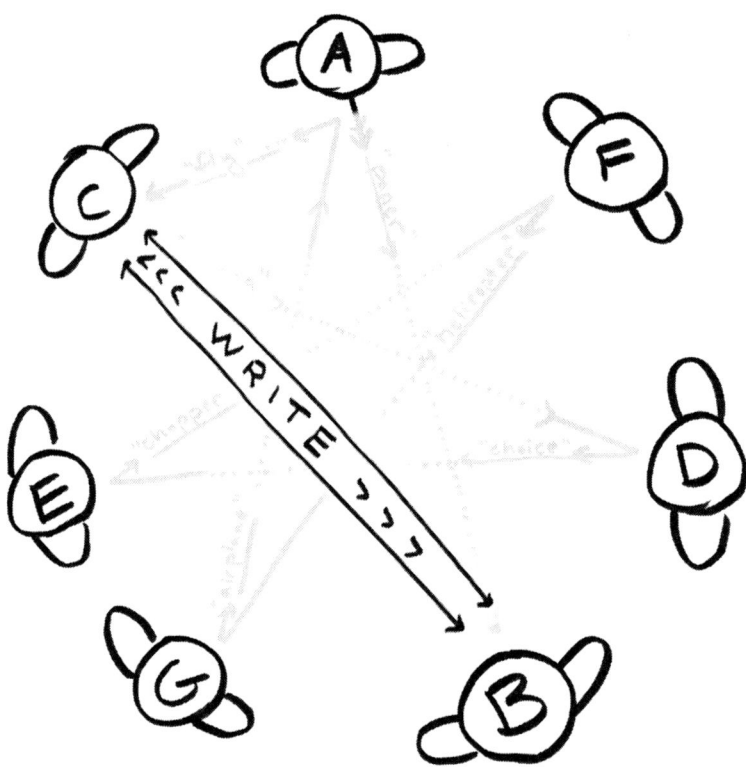

(You can go back and forth either way! That's how bridges work!)

Therefore, once the bridges are built going forwards, the leader can then run the pattern... backwards! Running the pattern backwards means crossing all the bridges in the opposite direction, so players are returning someone else's word back to them. Starting from the end of the previous example:

...
C to A: Fly
A to G: Airplane
G to F: Helicopter
F to E: Chopper
... etc.

Making it even harder: When you've practiced the pattern all the way through forwards and all the way through backwards, you can practice turning it around in the middle. The leader, or anyone in the circle, can reverse the direction of the pattern at any time, by repeating a word to send it back across the bridge in the other direction:

...
E to C: Fly
C to A: Airplane
A to F: Helicopter ...
F to A: Helicopter
A to C: Airplane
C to E: Fly
...

(Again, it's much easier to try it than to explain... Give it a go; it's a great mind-bender.)

MANDY KHOSHNEVISAN

Introduce your Neighbor

For: Ages 7 and up

character, circle, physicality

HOW TO PLAY:

Standing in a circle, one person introduces their neighbor to the rest of the circle: "This is my Great-Aunt Gladys, who's very tall and thin and speaks in a very high voice." The person now endowed as Gladys takes on the characteristics of that character, and (hopefully speaking in a very high voice, as dictated) introduces *their* neighbor. Continue around the circle (and keep going around, if you like). The characters should know each other (or how could they introduce each other?) so it's possible there's the hint of a story emerging as the game progresses, although there doesn't have to be a cohesive throughline.

Variations:

More Theatrical: You might have each character give a short monologue (30 seconds is plenty) after they're introduced, or once you've gone all the way around the circle. A "monologue" may sound daunting; you can tell them it's essentially a tirade or rant about something that character believes strongly. A monologue might start with a phrase like:

"Life is like a _____,"

"I'll tell you what's really important,"

"Always remember this,"

"As I always say,"

"You know what I love?"

"You know what I can't stand?"

For even more interaction, after everyone has a character and has performed a short point-of-view monologue, you might say, "Now, let's have a party!" and have the characters mingle with each other and interact for a while. You could declare the party to be a barbecue, a wedding, a funeral, a PTA meeting… any event where these characters might all meet each other. To get them to keep mixing and mingling, I usually tell them they should speak (as their characters) to everyone at the party at least once.

Creative Writing: Once everyone has been given a character, you might have everyone write something about their character, or from their character's point of view. It could be a letter to someone, a diary entry, a short monologue, a story in the first person, a reaction to another piece of writing, or you could have players write a story or play about that character.

Art: Suggestions to make this a visual art activity:

- Once everyone has been introduced as a character, and perhaps had a chance to talk a little about themselves or interact at a "party," they can draw a "self-portrait" of this new character.
- Everyone could draw a picture of a character first, and then stand in a circle. The artist could introduce their neighbor by showing everyone the portrait they drew; the neighbor would then take on the characteristics they see in the portrait: how that character stands, what face they're making, etc. While speaking and acting as this new character, they would then introduce *their* neighbor and portrait, and so on around the circle.

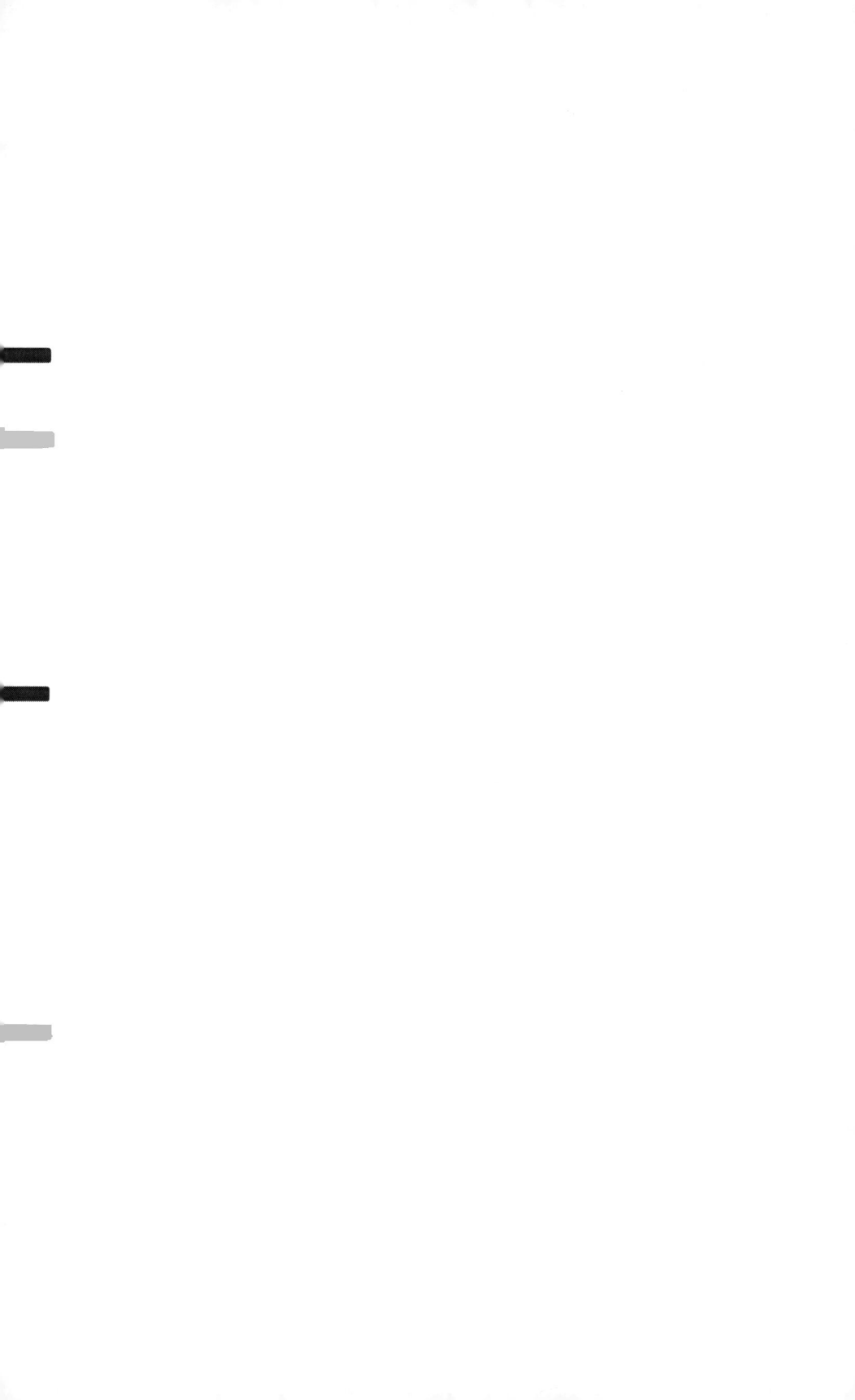

BALL GAMES

It's fun to play games in a circle, and it's fun to play ball! A lot of improv warmup games are played in a circle, and most of them with some sort of invisble "ball." It's a win-win! (If physicality is a skill you're working on, you can coach kids to pay attention to what kind of ball it is -- big or small? Heavy or light? -- and where in space it is; get them to treat it like a real ball that travels at real speed. Have them leave room in their hands for a ball, and get them to throw and catch it like a real ball.)

General Coaching Notes:

Often, small children — ages six and under — have trouble playing games where you have to toss a ball, especially an imaginary ball, across a circle. The question of who to throw it to can be overwhelming, and an imaginary ball is difficult for some younger children to visualize or keep consistent. If passing across the circle is slowing things down, you can use one or more of these strategies to start off with: 1. Instead of passing across the circle, just pass around the circle in order. 2. Use a real object to pass — something soft and catchable that doesn't bounce too much, like a small beanbag, a stuffed animal, or a Koosh ball. 3. Have them sit down and roll a real ball across the circle instead, with no throwing allowed.

MANDY KHOSHNEVISAN

BALL! (The one with a real ball)

<u>For: Everyone</u>

circle; group; physical

You've probably played this game before on the playground when you were a child, and had no idea it was teaching you improv skills. Often a physical challenge with a real object and simple stakes is a great way to create energized focus within a group.[1] Keith Johnstone has been known to maintain that a performing group's pre-show warmup should consist solely of kicking around a soccer ball for twenty minutes or so.[2]

HOW TO PLAY:

For the safety of players and surroundings, it's best to use a ball that's not too small, not very heavy, and not particularly bouncy. At Bay Area TheatreSports, the best ball we found was a soft inflatable indoor soccer ball, the kind that's made of fabric instead of leather or rubber. You could also use a beach ball or other inflatable plastic or rubbery ball. For very small children, you could use a balloon. (And you can definitely play this indoors, but it's also a great game for playing outside.)

Starting in a circle, you work together to keep the ball off the ground. These are the rules of "Ball":

---

1   Three For All, an extremely talented three-man improv theater group made up of Steven Kearin, Tim Orr and Rafe Chase often uses this game as their only performance warmup. I've seen them spread out through the entire theater while playing, jumping off chairs and diving across the stage. (And their actual shows aren't bad, either.)

2   He says this a lot while teaching; it's documented in my various workshop notebooks.

1. Everyone keeps the ball in the air by tapping or hitting it upward, not by catching it,
2. Everyone counts out loud each time the ball is hit upwards,
3. The ball can't touch the ground (you can make your own decisions about the wall or ceiling), and
4. One person can't hit the ball twice in a row.

When the ball hits the ground, when someone catches it, or when someone accidentally hits it twice in a row, the group starts counting again from "one." For a weekly class, I'll often make it a challenge to see if we can beat our current record.

Coaching Tips:

They may need some hints about the best way to hit the ball to keep it from going way too high or too fast. Depending on what kind of ball it is, you may want to urge them to tap it underhand like a volleyball, which will keep it up higher in the air. Hitting it overhand will cause it to shoot downward at people, which makes the game more difficult and possibly dangerous.

It's very important to discourage players from blaming each other for dropping the ball; after all, if the ball falls to the ground, in theory anyone could have saved it. You can point out to them: "Who says you have to stay in the circle? Who says you can't dive across the circle? Keeping the ball in the air is everyone's responsibility." Even if you've hit it once, and you know you can't hit it again right away, you can still help by scooting out of the way so someone else can get at it! When the ball hits the ground, if you get the ball back up in the air quickly, you can keep playing again quickly, and soon the times that the ball drops will not feel as important as the time the ball is spent in the air.

Focus on how long a run of volleys your group can count, and don't worry at all about how many times the ball gets dropped. Groups do get a lot better at this game, especially from week to week, so you may not want to spend too much time and energy setting a really high record the first time you play it. Give it maybe ten minutes, tops, the first time, and the next time you play it you'll have a relatively easy record to beat.

Gibberish Ball (and Gibberish Dictionary)

<u>For: Everyone</u>

pairs, circle, group

Sometimes improvisors speak in a language they call "gibberish"; this just means made-up words that sound like words.

How to Play:

Step one: say a made-up word, and point (or throw an imaginary ball) to someone else; the recipient should catch the ball and repeat the word as faithfully as they can. Then they make up a word and pass it to someone else, and round and round it goes.

Step two: when you're used to making up words and repeating them, you can make up definitions for them. The first person, as before, makes up a nonsense word and passes it to someone else. The recipient should repeat the word, and then tell everyone what it means, as if reading the dictionary definition.

> A: Blerpsnorp!
> B: Blerpsnorp: a kind of spoon made out of jelly! *[to someone else]*: Weeeeeeble!
> C: Weeeeeble: a small elf that lives in a teacup! [etc]

Coaching Tips:

You don't need to think too much, and you don't need to worry about it being too silly, or not sounding enough like a real word, or sounding

TOO much like a real word. Try doing this exercise without saying "filler words" while you're thinking, like "um" or "uh" ... challenge yourself to let the word leave your lips confidently and un-apologized-for. Since we're just making up words, this is a great game for practicing making a sound first and then completing the word as it leaves the mouth. "Trrrrrrrrr.. amboo!"

When trying to define someone else's word, again, don't think too much, and don't try to be too "clever"; think about what the word sounds like, and just say what seems to you like the obvious meaning, and that'll be fine. And if someone does, by accident, say a word that's a "real word?" Try to give it a nonsense definition, based on what it sounds like!

Sound Ball

<u>For: Everyone</u>

energy, non verbal, attention/ listening/ repetition, spontaneity, circle

HOW TO PLAY:

To pass the invisible ball in this game, you throw it and make a silly sound with your mouth. The person who catches it repeats the sound while catching the ball, and then throws the ball to someone else, making a different sound. It's fun to try out all the different sounds you can make (or didn't know you could make), and then it's also fun to try to repeat the crazy sounds that other people make. It's a good simple warmup for getting shyer kids out of their shells.

Coaching Tips:

Try to get players to imitate the sender as closely as they can — especially if it's a sound they wouldn't normally make. It's a sneaky chance to try on someone else's shoes, metaphorically.

If the sounds are starting to slide together and all sound alike, give some sidecoaching hints as you play, to see if you can challenge players to explore more. Think about what kinds of sounds they gravitate toward, and whether you can challenge them towards the opposite extremes. "Try to make a high sound! A low sound? Cast a spell! Can you make a sound that goes from high to low, or low to high? Make the sound of an emotion! Make the sound your pet makes! Make the opposite sound of the one you just caught!" Try anything that you think the group would enjoy.

First Letter, Last Letter Ball

<u>For: Age 7 and up (or younger players who are good spellers)</u>

energy, verbal, attention, spelling, pairs

HOW TO PLAY:

This is a word game: when you throw the energy ball, you say any word you like, and the catcher repeats it. To pass it on, you send a word that begins with the last letter of the word you caught, so it might sound like this:

"Fish!"
"Fish. Heaven!"
"Heaven. Naught!"
"Naught. Timing!"

There's no rule about whether the words have to be related or not; the only "rule" is the first letter-last letter connection.

Red Ball

<u>For: Everyone</u>

focus, energy, attention/ listening/ repetition, circle

HOW TO PLAY:

This is an invisible ball game that calls for focusing your attention. The first invisible ball is red; when you throw the red ball, you say "Red ball!" and to catch the red ball, you say "Red ball!" So it will sound like this, as you practice tossing it around the circle.

"Red ball!"

"Red ball. Red ball!"

"Red ball. Red ball!"

Pretty simple, eh? Practice that for a while, and then when people have gotten the hang of that, tell someone to hang onto the red ball, and then produce another ball, perhaps the yellow ball. Same thing: when you throw the yellow ball, you say "Yellow ball!" and when you catch the yellow ball, you say "Yellow ball!" Now, practice tossing around both at once. And, yikes! someone might get both at once! This isn't a crisis; just make sure they don't drop either ball, but catch and send each one deliberately. Now you see why you have to repeat the ball's name over and over: since it's invisible, the only way you know what color it is, is to say its name both on catching and throwing.

Got the hang of two? You can send around another one in another color. Make up as many as you want—and try to keep them all in the air!

The leader can pause periodically to catch them all, and if they all still exist and none were dropped, the group should celebrate.

Variations:

To make the game more of a mental or verbal challenge, you can toss some other kinds of balls into the mix: you could play with a red ball, a yellow ball, a blue ball, a sound ball, and a first-letter/last-letter ball all at once!

To make this game more of a physical challenge, you could vary the size and weight of the space objects you're passing, and to therefore make sure that the players honor that information and help keep it consistent. The red ball might be the size of an orange; the blue ball might be the size of a marble and very light; the yellow ball might be the size of a football (American or European)—or it might be the size and weight of a bowling ball. You can also add other space objects to the mix: we've passed around a refrigerator, a blow dart, a feather, a sneeze… use your imagination!

Zip-Zap-Zop

<u>For: Everyone</u>

circle; focus; memory; fast paced

This game is about keeping a pattern going, while sustaining the group's energy.

HOW TO PLAY:

Standing in a circle, you take turns passing the energy around: you can send it to anyone, whether they're standing next to you or across the circle. The traditional way to send the energy in this game is to shoot your flat hand out to someone else in the circle, brushing it past your other flat hand to make a clap along the way (try it and you'll see what I mean). The first person sends the energy to someone and calls out, "Zip!" That player sends it to someone else: "Zap!" Next "Zop!" and the pattern keeps repeating in that exact order: zip, zap, zop, zip, zap, zop. When the pattern derails somehow—someone says the wrong word, or hesitates for too long—you can have the whole group cheer "Pow!" (or some other fun thing to yell), and start over. You might add that on a "Pow!," everyone has to scramble to a new place in the circle, before beginning again.[3]

Variations:

Because repeating a pattern of just three words is not all that difficult, you can play a variation where you make up new patterns. (I learned this

---

[3] Some play this as an elimination game, though I don't find that a terribly interesting way to play.

at Curious Comedy in Portland; not sure where it's originally from.) To add a new pattern, when the "zip, zap, zop" sequence would repeat— when it's time to say "zip" again— someone could instead send a new word, which means it's a new pattern. The next two people add two more words in sequence to the new pattern, using word association:

A: Fish!
B: Sticks!
C: Rule!

Now there are two patterns: zip-zap-zop and fish-sticks-rule. You can continue playing with those two patterns until someone starts another one:

D: Donut!
E: Coffee!
F: Muffins!

Now there are three patterns.

Even harder: Once it feels like there are enough patterns going around, you can start playing a "Lightning Round," where there are no more new patterns, BUT you're not allowed to have two of the same pattern in a row. It might sound like this:

"Zip!"
"Zap!"
"Zop!"
"Donut!"
"Coffee!"
"Muffins!"
"Fish!"
"Sticks!"

"Rule!"
"Donut!"
"Coffee!"
"Muffins!"

Each individual pattern has to remain intact, but the patterns can happen in any order as long as there aren't two in a row that are the same. Now that it's a more ridiculous level of difficulty, you can either play with eliminations or individual or group forfeits — or with two circles playing at once, and when you trip up, instead of being "out," you just run to the other circle.

Bibbity-Bibbity-Bop

<u>For: Everyone</u>

circle; group; energy

This is one of those games that starts out with a basic set of rules, and then as the group plays it, sometimes over days and weeks, it can grow and evolve all sorts of fun and silly rules as the group creates them. As the group's facilitator, it's fun to lead that drive to make up new rules when they happen organically. Something that happens accidentally and organically, instead of being a "mistake," can become a new rule. You can add that to the list of "official" rules for your group, and then your group has its own special, custom-made game!

How to Play:

The game takes place in a circle, with one person in the middle. Their job is to get themselves out of the middle by causing someone on the outside to "mess up"; that person comes to replace them in the center. It's a call-and-response game: the person in the middle chooses someone on the outside, using eye contact, and based on what the person in the middle says, the person on the outside must respond in a certain way. The two basic default rules: if the person in the middle looks at someone and says "Bibbity-bibbity-bop," the chosen person must say "Bop!" before the person in the center has finished their phrase, or else they wind up in the middle. BUT! If the person in the center just says "Bop!" the chosen person can't say anything; any utterance at all and they wind up in the middle.

To this set of two tricky opposites, which are the default commands, you can add all sorts of other commands that the person in the center can issue to the players. You can add some three-person pictures, to be formed by the player being addressed, as well as their immediate neighbors on either side.[4] The pictures must be completed before the person-in-the-middle counts to ten. (I tell them, as long as you say all the numbers, you can count as fast as you can; it's not being "unfair.") If any one of the three doesn't make it by the ten-count, they wind up in the middle.

Some possible three-person pictures:

- **"Elephant!"**: The person who got "elephant" wraps one arm around the other to form a trunk (elephant sounds encouraged but optional); their neighbors on either side each make a big ear with their hands
- **"Jello!"**: The person in the center wiggles like jello, and the people to each side join hands around the jello to form the bowl.
- **"Viking!"**: The center person puts their hands up like a horned hat, and yells, "Arrrrgh!" The people on either side row the boat, chanting "Viking, viking, viking."
- **"Elvis Presley!"**: The person in the center grabs a microphone and says, "Thank you, thankyouverymuch," while the side people act like screaming fans.
- **"Winged Avenger!"**: The person in the center makes a superhero mask out of their hands (you know, that thing where you flip your hands upside down? you know.) and shouts, "I'll

---

4   There are endless regional variations of this game, and lots of different "standard" moves. My descriptions of them are just the ones I've learned from people, and you can really do them however you want.

save you!" while their neighbors each hold up their outside arm like a giant wing.

You can also use whatever other three-person structures you happen to know from other sources or games. You can even add an "all-play," where the person in the middle of the circle shouts a certain command, and EVERYONE has to perform something. Like, "Klingon Warrior!" Everyone puts their hands on their hips, steps forward, and says in a deep voice, "I am a Klingon warrior." Or, "James Brown!" Where everyone repeats, "Jump back *[jump straight backward]*, kiss myself *[kiss back of hand]*, unh *[hip thrust]*!" Or, you could make something up.

Because this game can take awhile to explain, I usually introduce rules in stages, starting with the two basic defaults and then maybe one or two of the three-person pictures. I might add another one in a few minutes, assessing the group as I go. This game can have as many rules or "commands" as the group can collectively remember, and the list can grow as you play it on multiple occasions, but it's best to start out with only a few.

Coaching Tips:

Since the person in the middle is the one in control of the game at any given moment, their individual performance can do a lot to set precedent for future players; I usually demonstrate first, to set up the expectation that the game moves quickly. The idea is for the person in the center of the circle should go FAST, without taking time to make decisions or think of something to do. I like to encourage them to go consecutively around the circle; this cuts down on the likelihood that they'll stand there and try to decide who they'd like to talk to. (One of the sneaky things about this game is that it forces the person in the middle to make eye contact with pretty much everyone, without making the eye contact itself a big deal.)

You can say more than one thing to a person, trying to psych them out: "Bop! Bibbity-bibbity-bop! Bop! Bop!" You can set up a pattern as you go around the circle and then break it, trying to trick the players around the circle. The idea is to keep a quick tempo, so that everyone must keep their focus on the game.

I like to make the person in the middle the judge of whether someone has "messed up" or not; this allows the players to run the game by themselves.[5] (Unless, that is, the person in the middle is sneakily abusing their power in order to remain in the middle... then you can politely intervene!) There's no way to really win or lose this game, so let them know that you're all trying your best to be fair, but sometimes it's unclear and the person in the middle is the judge, and no one's winning a refrigerator here anyway.[6] If someone has been picked to go to the middle of the circle, but they're feeling shy in that moment and won't go, I'll let them pick someone to go in their place.

Variations:

Once things are moving right along and players have gotten the hang of the rules, you can start adding in new options. The more three-person pictures there are to choose from, the more fun the game becomes. If you have ideas yourself, you can create new ones; chances are, the kids are already bursting with ideas and can help you make some up.

---

5   One difficulty with this game is that often when you play it with kids, EVERYONE wants to be in the middle. Therefore, they'll try to mess up on purpose, which is pretty annoying. I try to emphasize that that's as much like "cheating" as you can get with this game, since it's no fun if you don't try to play the game right. That's another reason to get the person in the middle to go FAST, so that following the rules and trying not to get caught out becomes its own fun challenge. Sometimes if it's a large group, I'll break it up into a couple of circles once everyone's got the hang of it, or else I'll put multiple people in the middle of one big circle, so that more people have a chance to cycle through as the leader.

6   Thanks, Paul Killam for the quote.

There's also the Wild Card option: the person-in-the-middle can look at anyone and call out anything that isn't already a rule, and count to ten. The selected person and their two neighbors must try to act it out, just like the other three-person pictures. For example, if someone called, "Zoo escape!" and then counted to ten, the three players have until ten to snap into a reasonable tableau of "zoo escape," each quickly joining in without discussion or hesitation. Maybe someone's a gorilla bending the bars, maybe someone sees the gorilla and decides to do that too; maybe the third person decides to be a zookeeper and yell, "Come back here, you animals!" The Wild Card is my favorite part of the game: the person's offer is usually immensely delightful, and the look of confused, joyful panic on the three players' faces at being presented with a random offer and a time limit, is simply amazing. As long as they do *something*, it probably counts as correct, and if the group falls in love with it, you've got a new rule to add to your collection.

Whoosh-Bang-Pow

For: Everyone

circle; group; energy

As far as "games that evolve their own rules" goes, "Bibbity-Bibbity-Bop" is one format, and this is the other. Many of the fun variations in "Bibbity-Bibbity-Bop" will work in this game. The difference in format is that, instead of someone being in the middle, this is more like a "ball" game, where the energy travels around the circle. Mixing elements from this game and the previous one together, and making your own rules and procedures for them, you can come up with your own glorious, custom-tailored, silly game.

How to Play:

Players stand in a circle. The energy travels around the circle with the following **basic motions:**

- **Whoosh:** Travels in one direction. Player says "whoosh" and swoops hands to the next person, in the direction of travel. If not interrupted, the "whoosh" will just travel from person to person around and around the circle in the same direction.
- **Bang:** Bounces the energy back the way it came. Player crosses arms over their chest in an "X" and says, "Bang!" and it bounces back to the person who sent it. If you "bang" a "whoosh," the "whoosh" travels back around the circle in the opposite direction now, until something else happens.

- **Pow:** Sends the energy across the circle, but NOT to the person right next to you. Player makes eye contact with someone across the circle and says "Pow!" shooting the energy across with an extended fist. The recipient can "whoosh" in either direction, "bang" to bounce it back, or do something else.

Variations:

There are many many different versions of this game, and different "skins," as it were, so that even the basic motions are altered to fit the theme. I've learned it with a "Dukes of Hazzard" theme, for example, where instead of "whoosh-bang-pow" there was a steering wheel to send it around, a screech of brakes to "bang" it back the other way, and to send it across the circle, the player's hand leaps up and across like the General Lee jumping off a cliff, while the player beeps the car's horn — namely the first few bars of "Dixie." In short, this game is pretty modifiable even down to the basic level, to fit your theme, your lesson, or your favorite movie. Stir in as many variations as you like, and even switch themes back and forth during the game, if you like! Here's a list of some more variations to get you started, some of which I learned, and some of which groups have come up with organically during gameplay:

- **Ramp:** Skips over the next person in the direction of travel, as if jumping over their head; scoot your hand around them and say "Ramp!" (You could also use "Oil slick!" and skid around them to do the same thing.)
- **Tunnel:** Skips the next *two* people in the direction of travel, as if it's going beneath them; dip your hand down and say, "Tunnel!"

- **Transporter:** You can squish it down as your hands go flat, and make an electrical transporter noise: "zhooop!" as the energy ball disappears. Someone, anyone, across the circle, will catch it, by putting their hands flat and "zhooop!"ing them apart as if the energy has been transported there, *Star Trek*-style; then that person sends it on.
- **Train:** Whoever has the energy ball says, "All aboard!" Everyone faces around the circle and "choochoo"s around for one complete revolution; when you get back, the person who started the train sends the energy on again, perhaps with a "whoosh!"
- **Freakout:** If the person calls, "Freakout!" everyone waves their hands in the air, freaks out, and finds a new place to stand in the circle. When the circle is reassembled, the person who started it "whooshes" the energy along to the next person.

More: If the energy is in your possession, you can create your own ways to pass it. Shoot an arrow? Pass a glass of water? Let a hawk fly from you to someone across the circle? You can also use elements from almost any other circle game: any of the rules from "Bibbity Bibbity Bop," especially the three-person pictures and all-plays. You can seamlessly morph into playing "Zip, Zap, Zop," gibberish ball, sound ball, or anything else that occurs to you — and then morph back into "whoosh!"

MAKING OFFERS WITH YOUR PHYSICALITY

12

Many of us learn to be self-conscious in our bodies, and don't want to look "weird." Often, one person's "normal" is another person's "weird," and vice-versa. These physicality-based games let kids practice moving their bodies confidently, in ways they may not be used to moving.

People young and old may have different personal movement challenges: perhaps they're not used to making big, bold movements; perhaps they have difficulty sitting still or making controlled movements. Games that encourage creative physicality, and following or mirroring others' movements, will let all players explore different kinds of in a way that feels safe.

Pass the Clap

<u>For: Everyone</u>

circle, teamwork, group, split second

This is a circle game (in its basic form, anyway) that is good for focus, rhythm, and snap decisions. I've played this with kids as young as five or six; it warms up the skill of paying attention and taking turns.

How to Play:

Stand in a circle. If tiny kids can't handle standing up without fidgeting, you can do this sitting in a circle instead. Either way, I usually prepare the group playing this for the first time by leading the entire circle to clap at the same time as me. "Watch me," I say, "and try to all clap at the same time. It should sound like we're only one person clapping." I'll lead them all to clap at once three or four times, being very clear and not trying to fake them out. It's important to lead with this simple, clear behavior: if you try to fake them out because you think it'll be "funny," or because it'll "prove they're paying attention," it will put players on their guard, and they'll try to fake each other out, which is directly opposite to the point of the game. Hands open, then clap. Simple as that.

Then, to start the clap moving around the circle, I'll say, "Now let's pass the clap around the circle, and we'll see how fast we can make it go." (This desire for speed will also hopefully circumvent the desire some people have to fake out their neighbor. If you don't even bring up the concept, not even to ban it, hopefully it won't even come up.) When you're passing the clap around, just two people will be clapping simultaneously: the sender, and the receiver. You, as the model, should start passing it by consciously turning your whole torso to the side and making eye contact with the next person, and very clearly clapping your hands together; your neighbor should watch you and clap at exactly the same time, to "catch" it. The receiver should in turn swivel to the side and pass it to *their* neighbor. As it travels around the circle, two people always are clapping at once, but not more than two. Round the circle it goes; see if everyone can keep a consistent rhythm. Go around again, and then maybe send it back in the opposite direction just for good measure.

Coaching Tips:

Sometimes players will clap extraneously when it's not their turn, either because there's a rhythm and they get accidentally swept up, or sometimes because they're being mischievous on purpose. Gently remind them that only two people should be clapping at once. If they're getting confused or distracted, take a second to have everyone breathe, shake out their hands, and recenter. Once again, challenge the group: "Can we make the clap go all the way around? How fast can we go? Let's really concentrate and work together!" Conversely, if they're doing well at the basic pass-around-the-circle and players are adding extra claps because they're getting bored waiting, try moving forward to the next step(s), outlined below.

Variations:

Step Two: Switching Directions It usually only takes a few times around the circle for players to catch onto the basic mechanism, and then you can add a level of difficulty. Now, when you receive the clap, you can either choose to pass it on along, or bounce it back the way it came—it just depends which direction you choose to send it. Again, each time the clap transfers, two people are clapping—so I clap once to receive it, and then again to send it, even if I'm sending it back to the person from whom I got it. During this round, the clap may bounce back and forth around the circle; it may consistently desert one section of the circle, and it may well get stuck between two people passing it back and forth forever... if things are going well and you have the time, that can serve as an opportunity to segue into:

Step Three: Across the Circle To add another level of complexity, you can now pass the clap to anyone in the circle, not just your immediate neighbors. Very deliberate eye contact helps greatly with this; you may also wish to lean your body towards the intended recipient. If the group gets confused, you can remind them to keep their hands ready, watch the clap go around, and make eye contact. Sometimes they feel like they need to "choose" who to pass it to; in cases like these, you can ask them to keep to a rhythm, so they can't stall while making the decision.

Step Four: Break Up the Circle For advanced groups, if they're getting the pass-across version, you can move on to the fourth stage: the circle can break apart, and people can wander through the space. Passing the clap still requires two people clapping simultaneously, though now everyone is wandering instead of stationary. The easiest person to pass the clap to will be the first person you make eye contact with after receiving it—remembering to keep the rhythm fairly constant. Everyone should be wandering at once, swirling through the space and keeping their eyes open for the clap. (The group may end up all moving basically in a circle again, so you can urge them to mix it up, walk against the flow.)

Clown Circle

<u>For: Everyone</u>

group, circle

This game functions as both a good name-learning game for new students (I certainly use it that way; it helps me learn names superfast if I have a physical action to associate with them), and also a way to get players to loosen up and move with confidence.

How to Play:

Step one: Set it up!

The group should stand in a circle. Each person takes a turn, going in order; it's best if you the facilitator start first, to set a loud, confident example. For each player's turn, they take one step into the circle, and say their name while making some sort of movement or gesture that's distinct from everyone else's movement so far. Hopefully they say their name confidently and loudly enough for others to hear, and the movement is distinct, repeatable, and physically safe enough for the whole group to attempt. After the person whose turn it is performs their name and movement, everyone else should repeat it, in unison. Then it's the next person's turn, and so on, around the entire circle.

Step Two: Review!

When everyone's had one turn, go around the circle one more time and quickly review, with everyone doing the same name-and-movement combination they did before. Person 1 goes, group repeats; person 2 goes, group repeats, and so on. After the review, I usually ask, "Does everyone remember at least their own movement and one other person's?"

Step Three: Play Ball!

Now the "energy," or the turn, or whatever you wish to call it, passes around the circle like you're throwing a ball (the whole group no longer repeats each name). As you start, you do your own name-and-movement, then someone else's. The "catcher" should repeat their own name-and-movement and then, to "throw" it, perform someone else's. Make sure that you cycle through everyone at least once before moving on to any variations.

Coaching Tips:

The movement should be something that everyone in the circle could reasonably approximate; human tricks like double joints or flying kicks are impressive, but are difficult for others to copy. If it's a movement that physical limitations prevent certain people from doing (like, say, the splits), just have everyone repeat it the best they can.

Sometimes children enjoy all eyes on them during this game, and sometimes they're shy about it. The important thing is that everyone feel successful and not damagingly embarrassed (especially if this is one of the first things you do), so any hesitation should be handled as smoothly and not-a-big-deal as possible. The goal is to quickly move from someone's turn to having the whole group repeat their name and movement and move on to the next person, thus not making anyone's turn a huge event.

If a player is having trouble thinking of a movement, as often happens, I always remind them "It doesn't have to be interesting, it just has to be

MANAGED MISCHIEF — MAKING OFFERS WITH YOUR PHYSICALITY

something," and I might give them some simple examples: jumping in the air, hopping on one foot, clapping hands, spinning around… anything that hasn't been done yet in the circle. If they happen to say their name loudly but refuse to move, I might pick up on a motion they're already doing: maybe they're shrugging their shoulders, or tapping their foot in a certain way. I'll say, "That! Should we do that?" and they'll often say yes.

If they're too shy to even say their own name loudly, I'll lean forward and ask them in a whisper, "What's your name?" and then repeat it so everyone can hear. Then I'll whisper to them, "What should we do?" They might feel safe physically or verbally suggesting a movement, but if they still look paralyzed, I'll make a few suggestions. "Should we jump in the air? Should we spin around?" They'll usually pick one of the given options, or be inspired to suggest their own. Then I'll say, "OK— on the count of three, everyone!" and we'll all do their name and the movement they picked, and then move on.

If a player is stymied by trying to decide who to send the energy to, you can suggest they do yours again; you can also remind the group with a smile, "If you're trying to remember someone's name, go ahead and ask them!" It's OK not to know what to do; it's important at an early stage of improv training not to make a roadblock into a long, awkward, big-deal standoff where everyone stares at the child who's having a block. I try my very hardest to breeze through such problems; it's OK to help them through it. If children get the sense early on that this improv thing will be hard, or make them embarrassed every time it's their turn, it may be harder to fix later. The goal is to gradually draw shy children out of their shells, so it's better to get them to participate in at least **SOME** part of their turn and making that perfectly OK, instead of allowing them to "pass" entirely. They'll get used to thinking they're an irredeemable failure and just shrink more and more and give up.

Variations:

One option, for older children or if you're focusing on the verbal, is to have everyone add an alliterative adjective to their name, when they're introducing their name and movement. And because it's more fun that way, you can frame it as a "superhero" adjective: "Dashing Derek!" "Marvelous Maisie!" "Stupendous Steven!"

There are also some variations for escalating the game, if they're having fun and you want to keep going.

- **Just Motions:** Once everyone seems to be getting it, you can pause and give modified instructions: now, leave the names out, and just do the motions that have been already established (this is why it's best to have everyone's motions distinct from each other). This is pretty fun, and will probably elicit a lot of laughter.
- **Secret Signals:** If you're feeling like it, you can step it up one more level, which is to try and send the movements as subtly as you possibly can, as if they were an accidental movement: a secret signal, one that might be mistaken for a random or unconscious movement if you weren't paying attention. Another way to think about making them more subtle is making them really "cool." For example, a player might try to disguise what in the full-out version of movement is "arms stretched out high overhead!" by pretending to yawn. See if you can keep making the movements smaller and more "natural" until they're barely perceptible. This will quiet down the group and focus them; watching everyone's studied nonchalance as they pass secret movements is a really fun and funny variation of the game.

MANAGED MISCHIEF — MAKING OFFERS WITH YOU

Fill the Space

<u>For: Everyone</u>

group, circle

I usually play this one right before I play Mirror, since it helps kids warm up to making big and oddly-shaped physical offers.

HOW TO PLAY:

Everyone stands in a circle. One person goes in the center and takes a pose and holds it. Their neighbor also enters the center area and "fills the space" around the first person, taking a pose somewhere inside the circle that somehow seems, to them, complementary to the first player's pose. Fast action is key here; it doesn't need to take more than a few seconds to take up an arbitrary position. The second person's pose doesn't intrinsically have to "mean" anything. The first person says "Thank you!" and exits, leaving the second person in the middle, still frozen in the same pose. A third person enters and fills the space; the second person says "Thank you!" and exits.... repeat around the circle. Often it's worthwhile to go around the circle at least twice, as players will be inspired by watching each other.

Coaching Tips:

As long as the person entering is somewhere in the circle, they're doing it right—they're filling the space. This game is about abstract shapes and positive and negative space, so there's no "right way" to fill the space. There may be ways to fill the space that are more fun than others, but they're not more "correct." Since the pose is arbitrary and abstract, you can encourage players to jump in fairly quickly, in order to support each other. (It's like a high-five: don't leave them hanging!) And whether or not the players have a specific relational idea in mind, as onlookers they may realize that our minds will create some sort of story or relationship between two people filling the same space. They don't have to have an "idea" going in; the onlookers will find one.

It's a very simple game, but going around more than one or two times may suggest new fun things to do, depending on what the players see happening during the first and second rounds. Maybe someone lies down on the floor, and that looks like fun. Perhaps there's a sequence where people stand back to back. Perhaps players decide to see what it's like to stand incredibly close to each other, or as far away as possible. This is one of those games that starts with one simple rule and nothing else, but using the muscle of "seeing what's happening," players can create something totally logical but totally unexpected.

Variations:

You could try having more than one person fill the space at once; see how many people can fill the same space without touching, perhaps.

Art:

You could pair the physical exercise with an art exercise: positive and negative space are also terms from visual art and composition. Positive space is the area taken up by a specific object or form, and negative space is the air, the nothing, around it. You could play "Fill the Space" with a giant piece of paper or a whiteboard, letting students draw shapes that interact using positive and negative space. If it's a whiteboard, you could erase the original shape, or you could leave all the shapes and try to fill up the entire available art surface.

MANAGED MISCHIEF — MAKING OFFERS WITH YOUR PHYSICALITY

You could even do this with three-dimensional art, as a group or in partners: have one person put together a sculpture, and have someone else add their own piece which interacts with the space around the first one in an interesting way. This would be a fun exercise to do with a changeable building material such as playdough or blocks, so that you can go back and forth: someone builds a sculpture, someone else builds a sculpture filling the negative space around the first one. Then you can take the first piece away, and examine the one left behind. Someone else is now free to fill the space around *that* piece, and so on.

Mirror

<u>For: Everyone</u>

pairs, focus, give and take, sharing control

The mirror exercise is a tried-and-true theatrical exercise that's fun to do, and it emphasizes observation and give-and-take.

HOW TO PLAY:

Partner up (it's easiest if the people are sort of the same size; it's a little more difficult to do with a small child and tall adult, but it can be done). If there's a moderator, have each partner group designate an A person and a B person. Partners should stand facing each other and put their hands up flat, as if on a mirror. (If it's proving confusing or difficult, you might start with both participants sitting on the floor.) Hands shouldn't be touching; there should be a little space between the two sets of hands, equivalent to the glass of the mirror. Explain that, just like with a real mirror, nothing should pass through the invisible plane between people. Before you let them loose to explore, you can explain some of the specific mirror mechanics: one person lifts their hand away from the mirror, the other person's mirror hand moves away too (instead of forward, through the mirror). The other reason to start facing with both hands up on the glass is to spatially reinforce the concept of mirroring: if the "person" lifts their right hand from the glass, the mirror image doesn't move their own right hand, but their left. Have the groups practice lifting a hand off the "glass" and replacing it, watching as the two mirrored hands move apart and then back together. Explain that the goal is not for the leader to make the other person "mess up" by tricking them; the goal is to be

MANAGED MISCHIEF — MAKING OFFERS WITH YOUR PHYSICALITY

so smooth and synchronized that it should be hard for an onlooker to guess who's leading and who's following. I usually say something like, "I'm going to walk around and watch you; see if you can be so smooth that I can't tell who the leader is!"

To start off, have A be the "leader" and B the mirror. A should lead the movements, and B should try to follow as exactly as possible ... facial expression, body posture, etc. Set all the pairs free to experiment, and you can wander around observing. After a minute or so, you can call "switch" and have B take over leading — ideally B should start with the position they're in when "switch" is called; they shouldn't drop to neutral and start with a "new idea." To emphasize starting from whatever position they happen to be in, you might want to call "freeze" and then "switch." Let the Bs lead for a while, and then switch again. Call switches gradually faster and faster if you wish. Switch partners, if you have a large crowd, and try the same again, prompting them to keep experimenting with different ways to move.

Coaching Tips:

I say this a lot: "Don't think too hard. It doesn't have to be good, it just has to be something." Sometimes people get hung up on thinking of a "good" movement, but really any movement at all will do. Just by standing there trying to think of something, they're already doing plenty of things. You can remind the follower to "see what's happening," and mirror everything about their partner, even facial expressions and head-scratching.

After a warmup period, you can introduce some sidecoaching about ways to explore different kinds of movement. Often participants will be fixated on circling their arms, and then run out of ideas. You can gently suggest how to include movement in other dimensions: moving closer or farther away from the mirror, leaning their torso/body to the side, bending their knees to move up and down, and even creating sideways movement. The mirror should stay in the same place, but they can travel side to side. If you're in a big room, challenge them to move as far apart as they can while still mirroring each other.

Variations:

This may possibly blow their minds, but I often try this as a one-minute coda on the end of our first mirror practice, and then come back to it later on another day. You can tell them, "Pretend that both of you are leading and both of you are following at the same time! Now, go!"[1] This will probably incur some incredulous looks, but they'll likely figure it out. Oftentimes a group will handle this confusing instruction by stopping to put their heads together and plan sequences of activities in advance; try to get them not to use verbal skills. To head off complicated plotting, you can say, "Everyone pretend that your partner is the leader, and try to mirror what they're doing! And yes, that means that you're each following each other." This will, hopefully, show them what it's like not to "come up with" ideas, but just to see something and agree with it. "Keep moving at the same time! You're both following each other!" Mirroring even your partner's unconscious action (smiling, sneezing, brushing hair away) will magnify it, and soon they'll be creating a feedback loop.

Once they've figured out the basics of following each other, partners can experiment with making intentional movements; as they start the movement of an arm or a leg, they should see how their partner is mirroring them and follow, at the same time. It's a difficult exercise to wrap one's mind around, and it often puts participants into a bit of an uneasy state, since they're "not sure what's happening." But this state of

---

[1] It's similar to Follow the Follower, on page 75, but somehow when it's just two of you it feels much more strange.

MANAGED MISCHIEF — MAKING OFFERS WITH YOUR PHYSICALITY

confident observant leading-and-following is a good place to put one's mind.

Mirroring-the-mirror is a visceral, immediate illustration of what it's like to create something with another person. Player A may reach out their arm with the intention of making a rainbow arc, but Player B, imitating that gesture, may think, Gosh, it looks like we're reaching for a glass of water, and, doing just what seems obvious, may reach for a glass of water and pick it up. Person A, mirroring that movement of picking something up, might think, Yeah, a ball! and steer their hand towards throwing it up in the air. It's like a human Ouija board... something is happening, which is being steered simultaneously by both people and neither person.

Dance: This can turn into a dancing activity; you can do the exact same exercise while set to music. Players can make a conscious effort to dance or move along to the music, or you can use the music just to set a mood.

You can also use group mirroring to make some fancy-looking improvised choreography. In Diamond Dance (page 234), the whole group is mirroring one person, but you can use mirrored pairs to create a more complex look. Pretend there's a mirror running down the center of the stage or performance space. A group of pairs arranges themselves on the stage in a reflected tableau, with the As on one side of the mirror, and Bs on the other side. Each person, therefore, has a mirrored counterpart on the opposite side of the center line. Silently or to music, everyone begins moving, while mirroring their partner across the stage. Pairs can move upstage or downstage, closer to the center or farther from it. People on the stage can interact with others on their side of the mirror or not. If everyone is concentrating on mirroring, the stage will look complicated yet unified; it's practically magic.

You can assign one side of the stage to be the leaders, let each pair decide who will be the leader (which means there will be leaders on both sides), or you can let each pair "follow the follower" and pass the leadership dynamically between them. You might let the music inspire the piece, or you might suggest a theme ahead of time. You can have all your players make a piece at the same time, or you can divide them into groups and let them watch each others' mirrored improv choreography.

MANAGED MISCHIEF — MAKING OFFERS WITH YOUR PHYSICALITY

I am a Tree

For: Everyone

group, audience, physical, freezing

This exercise was in theory brought to Bay Area Theatresports via… the Netherlands? Germany? Somewhere across the Atlantic, at any rate. Adults love this game; so do preschoolers!

How to Play:

Someone starts by posing in a tree-shaped pose and announcing, "I am a tree!"[2] The next person joins them and poses as something else, *anything* else that seems to belong in that tableau, and then announces what they are: "I am a bird!" for example. Now the picture has a different flavor: a tree and a bird. A third person joins and becomes something else that seems to belong in this new picture, which so far contains a tree and a bird: "I am a nest," say.

The person who started this original picture (in this case, the tree) makes a decision of who will stay and who will go, and announces it: "I'll take the nest." In this case, the tree and the nest rejoin the group of observers while the bird stays, still in its current pose, and announces again, "I am a bird!" It's now a new picture, this time starting with a bird. Trying not to just recreate the previous picture, someone else might enter and say, "I am a worm!" The third person might say, "I am the sun just rising!" The bird says, "I'll take the…" and so on and so on.

---

2   The beginning with a tree is arbitrary; it's just a place to start the whole game off and give the game a catchy name. Only the first tableau needs to start with a tree—and you don't even need to do that, if you really don't want to.

Coaching Tips:

Make sure the players are really, really taking turns, paying attention and giving each other space. There's room for everyone to contribute, but they must respect each other's space, both figurative and literal. Remind them: they must wait to enter until the previous person has created a pose and announced what they are.

If you have the opposite problem and players are being hesitant, you can remind them that they don't need to enter with a "good idea" or even any idea at all. If they follow their body into the stage space, an idea will come. For hesitant players, you can just have them play in order, down the line. Sometimes they need to have an excuse in order to prompt themselves into the game: "I *have* to go up, I guess, since I'm next."

This game is ripe for bringing up the concept of, "Hold on tightly, let go lightly": someone may be holding what they think is an amazing idea for something to add to the tableau. But if the person right before them creates something that changes the reality entirely … it's OK for them to let go of their idea in favor of a new idea that supports the new reality. The goal is to create a tableau of things that go together, not a set of three unrelated things. When playing, it's better to pay attention and contribute something that will support the collective creation, than to be thinking so hard about your own idea that you contribute something that will just be confusing, and—because you weren't paying attention—irrelevant.

Variations:

Once the group has gotten the hang of the three-person version, you can expand the picture to as many people as are inspired to join it—even everyone! Make sure they take turns, and wait until the previous person has found their pose and announced what they are before the next person

MANAGED MISCHIEF — MAKING OFFERS WITH YOUR PHYSICALITY

adds themselves to the picture. The first person can then say, "I'll LEAVE the…" and name the one who should remain to start the next tableau.

A more advanced variation is to steer the game a little more, focusing on categories or genres… you might say, now let's do tableaux about fairy tales, or superheroes, or sci fi movies, or another descriptor or restriction.[3] In general, adding restrictions often makes these kinds of games easier, so you might resort to that earlier, if you find them just repeating the same picture over and over (like my three- and four-year-old students… I had one class that just wanted to make nests and be eggs in them, over and over and over and over…They loved it, and it was really really cute; what can you do?)

Speaking of little children, I've found that for children up until about age six, they have a harder time with wanting to relate their pose to the rest of the picture; they just want to make a pose and tell everyone what they are. For a recent class, I made this tableau game a part of entering the room for drama: They would all wait at the door, and when I deemed them ready, I'd tap them on the head. Once tapped, they were to come in, put backpacks and shoes against the wall, and then go to the center of the room and become part of the tableau, which had a different theme every day. When everyone was in the room, I would go around and tap each one (starting with the ones who were frozen and quiet) and they could tell me what their pose represented. Once I'd asked everyone, I could let them release energy in a controlled way by unfreezing these creatures and freezing them again a few times, before transitioning to circle time or to the next activity.

---

3 This would be a great exercise to prepare for creative writing, especially if you're working on genres and story types.

Transformation Circle (Copy/Paste)

<u>For: Everyone</u>

circle, physical, vocal

This is another circle warmup, focusing on attention, "listening with your eyes," and verbal/physical exaggeration.

How to Play:

Everyone stands in a circle; the person starting the game turns to their immediate neighbor and performs some sort of physical gesture with an accompanying vocalization. The vocal part could be a word, a sound, a phrase, basically anything produced with the voice. (Don't think too hard; any choice is a fine choice.)

The first player delivers that sound-and-movement to their neighbor. The neighbor should watch, absorbing all the details of the sound and movement, and then turn to the next person and replicate what they just received. The third person observes, then turns to their neighbor and replicates that new version of the sound and gesture. The sound-and-movement travels all around the circle, and it can go around and around and around until it feels like the end.

Coaching Tips:

Players should be encouraged to try and faithfully reproduce what they were *just given* by the person before them. There are two basic forces working against this: someone makes a decision to consciously change the movement, or else someone wants to do it "right," so instead of

MANAGED MISCHIEF — MAKING OFFERS WITH YOUR PHYSICALITY

seeing what they were just given, they try to replicate the *original* sound and movement.

People tend to deliberately change the movement when they're having a high-status moment: they either want to be subversive, and take control by adding their own "crazy" movement instead; or else they're feeling embarrassed and make the movement and sound smaller. You don't need to specifically call out people for this kind of behavior, but you can notice it (and clearly all the other players will notice it as well). The person who's trying to do it "right" is probably the type that's anxious to follow directions, and gets annoyed when they feel other people aren't.

For both kinds of behavior, you can remind everyone of the original directive: "Try and see how exactly you can repeat what the person *right* before you did! Which arm did they use? Which leg? Which way did they lean?" and then as it changes, "Watch how the sound and movement seems to change by itself!"

Variations:

You can lead this game with different emphases to warm up different skills. You can play this game sending the same sound-and-movement around and around the circle several times, watching how it morphs and changes through time and repetition. You can also play a quickfire version, where everyone gets to make up their own sound and movement: Person A starts the sequence and it travels around the circle once, ending with Person A again. Then Person B starts a *new* sound and movement, which travels once around the circle and back to Person B. The next person starts a new one, and so on.

The "duplicate exactly!" instruction works for players who will benefit from practicing their focus and attention skills, so that it's more clear to the circle how a movement will morph gently even when we're not consciously trying to change anything. For a different approach, you can challenge them to observe the sound and movement, and then pass along a *slightly exaggerated* version of it. This will let it get weirder a lot faster, so it may provide more extreme physical and vocal gymnastics, which is always fun.

Copy/Paste: This is a version of the Transformation Circle; instead of passing the sound and movement to your neighbor, you walk across the circle to send it to someone, and then take their place. They in turn pick up the sound and movement, slightly exaggerating it, and choose someone else to take *their* place. This is a fun chance to practice silly walks and other ways of moving.

MANAGED MISCHIEF — MAKING OFFERS WITH YOUR PHYSICALITY

Boom, Baby!

For: Everyone

circle; physicality; attention; memory

I learned this game very recently, and I have no idea why it's called Boom, Baby! except that it's a fun thing to say. That's reason enough! This game is a little like "Pass the Clap" (page 172) except that instead of simultaneously clapping, players are simultaneously repeating a sound and movement pattern.

How to Play:

Players stand in a circle. The leader suggests a general topic or idea: "Space," for example. Then players establish their pattern. The first person (A) turns to their neighbor (B) on one side, and creates a sound (verbal or non-verbal) and movement that have something to do with space. Maybe they take a big step and say, "One small step for man!" Whatever the sound and movement, they perform it once for their neighbor, and then the two players repeat that same sound and movement together. Then B turns to C and creates another space-related sound and movement. Maybe they pretend to be weightless and say "I'm floating!" B performs it once for C, and then they repeat it together. C creates something for D, and so on. Repeat the process around the circle, so that everyone's established a sound-and-movement.

Now that the pattern is established, repeat it again in the same direction around the circle. This time, every action is performed by both participants at once:

A and B: "One small step for man…"

B and C: "I'm flooooatingg!"

C and D: "Three, two, one, blastoff!" etc.

Keep going around the circle in the same direction to cement this pattern.

Variations:

There are two different avenues to adding another step of difficulty.

First, you can allow players to change the direction of the pattern. When receiving the pattern—performing a sound and movement with their neighbor—a player can either turn to their other neighbor and together perform the next sound and movement, or they can stay facing the same direction and repeat the one they just did, bouncing the pattern back around in the other direction:

A and B: "One small step for man…"

B and C: "I'm flooooatingg!"

C and D: "Three, two, one, blastoff!" etc.

[D decides to send it back the other way, so doesn't turn to E and instead:]

D and C: "Three, two, one, blastoff!" etc.

C and B: "I'm flooooatingg!"

B and A: "One small step for man…"

The other way to go towards creating more silly chaos is to save the first pattern in your memory, and create a different pattern in the other direction: if your first one was "Space," maybe the second one is "Dinosaurs." Travelling in the opposite direction around the circle, establish this second pattern using the same method as the first one: Person A turns to person G and performs a sound and movement: "T-Rex Smash!" and then they repeat it, this time in unison. Person G

MANAGED MISCHIEF — MAKING OFFERS WITH YOUR PHYSICALITY

turns to person F and creates another dinosaur combination, and so on around back to A.

Once you have two patterns, you can send them both around the circle in opposite directions. This means that twice in every rotation someone will get both at once; it's fun to see how these points of crossing shift as you play.

If you were really feeling crazy, you could even try both variations at once, and let both patterns move around the circle with players being able to shift directions ... that would be the Super Advanced way to play, but it might be just right for your group of players.

MANDY KHOSHNEVISAN

Match My Rhythm

For: Everyone

music; rhythm; physicality

How to Play:

Sit or stand in a circle, and establish a basic steady beat at a fairly slow tempo. It works best to clap on knees, then hands together; knees, then hands together. Have the whole group establish this beat and clap it together. Then, the players can start taking turns around the circle: each person will create their own rhythm that's the same length as four counts, or one "measure": the time it takes to clap, "knees, hands, knees, hands." The person whose turn it is claps (or snaps, stomps, slaps, etc) their rhythm, and then the whole group tries to repeat it exactly. To cement and perfect that measure's worth of rhythm, you can do it two ways:

Leader: (Boom boom bah, boom boom bah!)
Everyone: (Boom boom bah, boom boom bah!)
Leader: (Boom boom bah, boom boom bah!)
Everyone: (Boom boom bah, boom boom bah!)

This way is a double call and response; solo, repeat; same solo, repeat. You could also have the whole group repeat it three times together:

Leader: (Clap clap stomp, snappity stomp!)
Everyone: (Clap clap stomp, snappity stomp!)
(Clap clap stomp, snappity stomp!)
(Clap clap stomp, snappity stomp!)

MANAGED MISCHIEF — MAKING OFFERS WITH YOUR PHYSICALITY

In either variation, the entire exchange takes up four measures, or four sets of four counts. Then the next person in the circle creates a rhythm, which is repeated by the group in your chosen pattern, and so on around the circle.

Coaching Tips:

Just like when you're creating anything together, you can encourage players to look for the "game" that seems to be emerging, and see if they can help it happen, or play around with the "rules" that seem to be appearing. Is everyone only using their hands to make sounds? How else can you use your hands to make sounds? Can you use your feet instead? What about other parts of your body?

Variations:

Voice: Players could add their voices to the range of physical "instruments" available to them.

"Real Instruments": Players could even try this with actual musical instruments; everyone could have a different instrument with which to create and repeat rhythms.

Phrases: If you're playing with the call and response pattern, you could have each rhythm leader make two slightly different rhythms during their turn: two related phrases, like a question and answer:

Leader: (Clap clap clap, snappity snap?)
Everyone: (Clap clap clap, snappity snap?)
Leader: (Clap clap clap, snap snap clap!)
Everyone: (Clap clap clap, snap snap clap!)

Morphing Space Object Circle

For: Age 7 and up

circle, partners, silent, physical

A bit of jargon: it's fairly common in improv circles to refer to invisible onstage objects as "space objects": objects made of space. If your group can give attention to the idea of playing with invisible objects, it gives everyone more of a common physical language, and more opportunities for playing fun games. With space, you can conjure up anything you need, right away! Plus, no one can get hurt with a space-object sword.

HOW TO PLAY:

Someone starts with a nebulous ball of space in their hands. They pull and stretch it until they form it into a specific object. They mime using the object, in order to make clear to everyone what it is, and then pass it to the next person. The next person takes the object, honoring its current shape. This next player also interacts with the object in its current form; then they can pull and push and stretch it into a different object. They'll use that object as its own form, then pass it to their neighbor. Repeat all the way around the circle. (Or play with a small group or in partners.)

Coaching Tips:

This should be a silent game; players can make sound effects for their object if absolutely necessary, but you shouldn't use words to play. Encourage players to keep the size, shape, and weight of each object consistent, so that their fellow players can clearly see what it is. The clearer it is to us what the object is, the more fun opportunities we can think of to play with it.

Whenever I've played this game, the participants are silent and riveted. No matter how much adults ridicule mime, in my experience kids are absolutely fascinated by it. I'm always surprised every time I quiet down a fractious group of kids by miming an invisible wall. (It happens from time to time that I run into one of my past students in some public place, maybe even a student from years earlier—and surprisingly often, that student will make themselves known to me by running up to me and miming an invisible wall. Seriously! They **LOVE MIME**.)

Spacewalk

For: Everyone

physical, group, energy, space

HOW TO PLAY:

This exercise is about moving, as yourself, through an imagined environment. Scatter people around the space; players should stay in their own "space bubble" and not touch or interact with each other. If you like, you can start out letting them move around the space normally, walking through the regular air. After a few seconds, I like to call "freeze," and usually clap to help gather everyone's attention. Then, name a type of environment they're walking through instead, and let them explore what it would feel like: peanut butter, water, fog, cotton candy, glue…

Coaching Tips:

As they move, you can sidecoach: What does it feel like? What does it smell like? Dig your fingers into it; roll around in it; move faster! Move slower! Try to sit down! You can name different body parts: how do you move your knees through peanut butter? How about your eyelashes? Make suggestions in order to remind them to engage their entire body, and to surprise them into thinking of something they didn't think to think about.

Statues
(Wax Museum; Museum Guard; Haunted Museum)

For: Everyone

group; physical; freezing

HOW TO PLAY:

All the players spread themselves through the space and find a place to become a "statue." If it's a fairly large space, it's often helpful to designate a discrete area to function as the "museum." One player is chosen to be the Museum Guard; that player waits outside the museum space. When leading the game, give the other players time to find a place to be still, and then ceremoniously lead the guard into the museum ("I hear it's haunted…"). Once the guard is in the room, the game has begun: if the guard is not looking at them, the statues can move around—but when the guard looks, the statues should be completely frozen.

If the guard catches any statues in the act of moving, the guard should point it out; those statues in question should then commit a "forfeit." Some sets of rules call for those players to be "out"; I like to play that they have to theatrically explode into dust, and then lie on the floor, after which they can reform into statues. (You might want to give them a time limit: set a timer, or count out loud to ten or twenty or thirty, after which the statues can reform.)

Coaching Tips:

Man oh man, do kids love this game. In my experience, once you've played it, that's all they want to play. (It makes a very effective carrot.)

Because this is a game that really physicalizes failure, I like to praise players for their big, daring moves when the guard's back is turned. If played a certain way, this game can reward those kids who choose to stand in the corner or lie on the floor and never move at all; I prefer to champion those who push the limits and see how brave they can be in the face of elimination. If I see someone make a large move, whether they're caught or not I'll let them know I noticed: "Oh Tiffany, you dove right across the whole room! That was so brave!"

I make the guard the ultimate arbiter, careful to remind them that they can only call out people who they actually SEE moving, not who they *know* must have been moving merely because they've changed position. This way, they carry the responsibility of being "fair." On the flip side: because no one ever wants to feel like a fool, the guard is likely going to try and figure out a way to be looking at all the statues the whole time. But that's no fun! Coach them to turn their back to the whole group, and then suddenly whip around! Wary guards also like to circle the statues, keeping their eyes on the whole group; instead, urge them to wander through the middle of the museum, with statues both in front of them and behind them, and then weave through the group, making it less obvious when they're going to be turning or looking in any one direction.

The statues, in turn, often end up trying to get as close as possible to the guard, following them or even trying to touch them. I remind them, "If you make noise or touch the guard, they're going to know you're there and turn around! Be sneaky; don't let the guard know you're there!" You might remind the statues that they're playing a "game": their movements can start out small, and then get larger and larger as the game goes on.

MANAGED MISCHIEF — MAKING OFFERS WITH YOUR PHYSICALITY

Variations:

Because so many of my pre-K through elementary school students LOVE this game so much, I've toyed with altering the parameters in order to amuse myself, and also to focus on different aspects of the game.

This one's a game that you might try playing with actual eliminations, since this game is pretty fun to watch even if you're eliminated. Or to soften the blow, you could make the eliminated kids something inanimate that can't move anymore that would still belong in the museum ... maybe they're part of the wall? Maybe they're a gargoyle stuck to the wall? You also don't need to play until everyone but one person has been eliminated; you could set a timer for each round and see how many players can stay in after two minutes, or three minutes. That would also give more people a chance to be the guard, since pretty much everyone wants to be. (I've tried it with multiple guards in the same "room," and I just couldn't find a way to make it work. You could, however, set up two museums, each with their own guard, and have players switch to the other museum whenever they're called "out.")

For some of my preschool classes, I played that when you were "eliminated," you had to lie on the floor (or you could lie on the floor just if you felt like it), and when everyone was lying on the floor, the statue-ghosts would rise up all at once and chase the guard out of the room.

To make it even more of a focused movement game, for each round you might have the kids suggest what KIND of museum it's going to be, and make statues that would belong in that museum. Then you could challenge them to move the whole time like their statue would move (a statue of an animal would move like that animal, for example).

For even more focused movement, the guard can also "activate" statues by pushing the "on" button on their heads. When that happens, the statue momentarily comes to life and makes a small movement and sound, returning exactly to its position when it's done.

I've seen it suggested that this game be played in the dark (inside or outside) with flashlights... that seems like it would have fun potential. You would only be "caught" if you were seen moving through a flashlight beam.

You could also create more of a storyline, or set the main premise of the game—that people have to freeze when someone's watching them—in another location or within a larger story. One of my classes recently came up with a scenario where there were spies trying to steal some treasure; when the guards were in the room checking on the treasure, everyone had to freeze and/or hide behind something invisible, until the guards left again. You could make it into a storyline, where the treasure is supposed to end up stolen — or you could make it into a game, where the spies have to start on the edge of the room, make it to the center, steal a treasure, and make it out the "door" without getting caught moving. If the guard sees them moving, they have to put the treasure back and start from the beginning.

Opposites (or, Character Movements)

<u>For: Everyone</u>

physical, group, energy, space

This exercise is about moving as if you were a character entirely different from yourself, with a distinctive style of movement. Keith Johnstone created what he calls Fast Food Laban, based on the movement analysis work of Rudolf Laban; when working with children, I expand it some more, and call it Opposites.

HOW TO PLAY:

As with the Spacewalk, scatter everyone around the room to find their own space bubble. You can have players start out walking normally, and then freeze them. Then, give them a specific quality of movement, and have them explore the space as a person or creature who would move in that way. Initially, it's ideal if that kind of movement has an opposite, so you can have them switch to the other extreme. Feel free to experiment with different opposites of movement: Keith's Fast Food Laban categories are: Heavy/Light, Fast/Slow, and Direct/Indirect,[4] but those might be a little abstract for young folks, so you could also use opposites like Tall/Short, Old/Young, Big/Little, Solid/Liquid, Fire/Ice, etc. You can use anything you can think of, even if it's more abstract than concrete; players' interpretation of abstract concepts (Red/Green?) might be fascinating and fun to play with. (Laban's work is more about a continuum of movement quality, but we're interested in having students

---

[4] Direct: bodies and limbs moving the most efficient way possible, in straight lines. Indirect: moving in the most inefficient, wandering way possible.

explore extremes of movement; plus, children are interested in exploring opposites.)

Coaching Tips:

In Spacewalk we're pretending to be ourselves, but in this kind of exercise, we're actually making our body into another being as it moves through the world. The idea is that this new strange creature is *accustomed* to moving in each particular way. When we do "heavy," kids will tend to fall on the floor; I try instead to make them think that their creature IS extremely heavy, like a stone giant. Through every quality of movement, I sidecoach as we go, prompting them to stay present in their bodies: "Your fingers are light! Your knees are light, your elbows are light, your hair is light, your thoughts are light. Can you sit lightly? Can you stand still lightly? Can you touch the wall lightly?" Like with Spacewalk, I try to keep their full bodies engaged.

Variations:

Once you go through a series of opposites, you can see what it's like to do two — or more — at a time, from different pairs of movement extremes. I usually start with giving them two specifics: "This time when I unfreeze you, your whole entire body is going to be FAST, *and* LIGHT." After a minute or two, you could try the opposite: SLOW and HEAVY. You could mix it up: SLOW and LIGHT. Then you can present two categories and let the players decide what movement style: "This time when I unfreeze you, you can choose to be fast or slow, AND direct or indirect." Three kinds of movement at once might be the limit.

If it's a group that can handle it, after we've been going for a while, I'll have them start to interact lightly; I'll pause them and say, "When I unpause you, start to say hello to the people you pass, in this character's voice." These movement-based characters are often delightfully weird, and I love watching them interact.

If your group creates characters that they really like, you might try having a "party" with them so that all the characters can mingle and converse. You might also want to interview each of them in front of the group; they might have interesting and hilarious things to say.

Art/Creative Writing:

This game might even be a way into creating a character to draw or write about. You might ask players if they had a favorite kind of movement, and then ask them, "What do you think that character is like?" A character who is slow and light might be a balloon person, or they might be a fairy, or a person in space, or a kid fascinated by the world around her. Inhabiting another character's way of movement may give your players insight or inspiration that they weren't expecting.

Dance:

You could use these movement extremes specifically in a dance context, to music or not. Starting with a theme (summer?), you might ask players what kind of movement that suggests? Lightness, perhaps? Quickness? You might have them improvise a dance about summer, using the lightest and quickest movements possible. Could they dance about summer using the opposite kind of movement — heaviness and slowness? What if the dance about summer transitioned from light and quick to heavy and slow, or vice versa? What if it was a dance duet, starting with a light quick dancer and a heavy slow dancer?

There's a great, out-of-print book called *First Steps in Teaching Creative Dance*, by Mary Joyce, in which she lays out how to teach explorational dance lessons for young children. Her method is based around breaking down movement into abstract elements, teaching each new movement as a separate lesson that builds on the last one, and then encouraging children to explore those different movements and qualities. She writes,

> Dancers must begin at the beginning. They must first learn what the body can do, and how it can be done. Art grows from exploration, experimentation, and creative use of its elements. [...] When they become familiar with movement as a distinct and separate area of expression, not just an interpreter for dramatic action, then they will know dance. When they know how to work with the elements of the art, they can attempt to build a dance *about* an idea or image.[5]

Separating "quality of movement" from simply "miming a story" is an excellent way to get students, especially young students, to think about dance in terms of the actual kinds and qualities of movements used, and how movement evokes meaning and emotion, not the other way around. Emphasizing dance in this way, starting with the abstract, may make the concepts of choreography and even dance appreciation more accessible to young students.

---

5   *First Steps in Teaching Creative Dance*, p. 30.

Find the Thing

<u>For: Everyone</u>
physical; stage

Find the Thing is a natural extension of exercises like Opposites or other character movement exercises. I developed the specifics of this exercise for kids' classes, based on various physicality and clowning exercises I've learned.

How to Play:

First, you have to designate a "thing." I use a small orange Koosh ball (which are hard to come by these days, so kids are doubly fascinated with it). It doesn't really matter what it is, but for most purposes, and especially starting out, the Thing should be smallish (probably not smaller than a fist), simple, unbreakable (and also unlikely to cause terrible harm to others) and not *terribly* interesting in itself. You could use a small ball, or a wooden or plastic block; even a crumpled-up piece of paper would work.

Then, we take turns "finding" it. I get the participants into a line, so that they move through in order. The line faces the stage space, so that while waiting in line they're also the "audience." The first person enters the stage space as a character that moves in some way that's very different from their own personal way of moving. They could use a quality of movement they enjoyed from the Opposites exercise, above, or they could take on the characteristics of a specific animal, or they could just invent a really silly walk.

Using this new character walk, and therefore embodying a distinct character, the first player enters the space and walks around a little, exploring their new and weird movement style. Then they discover the Thing (you can place it somewhere on the stage space before you begin). It's nice if the player has some sort of emotional reaction to the Thing. This first weird creature picks up the Thing and can play around with it, still in character. A second player enters with their own weird character walk. The first player says "Hello," to the second player (in whatever voice their character seems to speak in). The second player says "Hello" back, in their own character voice. Then the first player must give the Thing to the second player, either directly, or by putting it down on the ground for them to pick up. Again, it's fun if one or both of them displays some kind of emotional reaction to transferring the Thing. Then the first player exits the stage space. The remaining character stays onstage, maybe walking around, maybe playing with the Thing. A new "second" player enters, and the scene happens again. Repeat, all the way around the room.

Coaching Tips:

In my experience, this doesn't require a whole lot of explanation beforehand in order for kids to just start playing this game. Some things to keep in mind while playing: it should be non-verbal, except for the two "Hello's". They can make emotional noises (sighs, grunts, laughter) but shouldn't converse. Also, the first person MUST give the Thing to the second person; if we're going to agree to play this game, we've got to agree to play it constructively. Even if the *character* gives up the Thing reluctantly, the *actor* should know that fulfilling the "contract" of this scene, so to speak, and letting it move forward, means completing the agreed-upon action. Because watching two characters fight isn't interesting. (And they should be discouraged from, say, *throwing* the Thing at each other—but you probably knew that.) Sometimes I'll convey the concept by sidecoaching, "You have to give it to them! That's how this story goes!"

It's a lot of fun when the characters have big emotional reactions, to the Thing or to each other; you can encourage them to explore more of that. Some characters may be naturally drawn to each other, and some characters may be naturally afraid of each other. As an advanced step, you can also encourage them to have that reaction while approximately facing the audience: watching a nonverbal exercise, we're primarily dependent on what we can see to determine what's going on and to figure out the relationship between the two characters.

Variations:

If this game is a hit with your players, you might want to make the "Thing" more complicated or larger, so that your characters have a more challenging thing to discover. You could use a chair, for example, or a simple everyday object that has more movement possibilities, like a book you can open and close, or a musical instrument that makes a sound. Having a more complicated or breakable object requires players to be more careful, so it's probably more of an advanced step, but it will be delightful to watch bizarre creatures discover the surprising qualities of simple objects.

Imaginary Environment

<u>For: Age six or seven and up</u>

group; space object; mime; memory; storytelling; building together

How to Play:

Players are going to build a space-object environment together, piece by piece. For the first few times, you can clearly state beforehand what kind of environment it is: a zoo, an office, a science lab, a superhero lair… The first player enters the room. (Bonus: because they're entering the room first, they can create a fun kind of door or entrance that everyone else should use also.) Then the first player creates a specific object in a specific location. They should "touch" it with their hands, showing everyone where it is, how big it is, how the moving parts (if any) work. You could play this with two levels of difficulty: the "easier" way to do it is to let the students announce what it is, while they're showing us where it is and how it works: "Here's a lion cage, and here's the door, and it opens like this." A more advanced level of difficulty, focusing more on their mime skills alone, is to limit them to nonverbal cues only—hands, body movements, and sound effects—to convey what the object is and how it works. The first person then exits.

A second player now enters the space (using the same entrance as the first player), interacts with the first person's object (like the lion cage) in some way, creates their own object or part of the environment, and then exits. The third player enters, interacts with the first two things, creates

MANAGED MISCHIEF — MAKING OFFERS WITH YOUR PHYSICALITY

their own thing, and exits. Repeat, through all the players (or as many as you'd like in this first round).

Coaching Tips:

This is yet another instance where it's good to remind everyone not to think too terribly hard, and that the object they're creating doesn't have to be the weirdest, most unexpected, most amazing thing in the world. If it's a schoolroom, there are some obvious objects that might be there (desks, chairs, whiteboards) and those things are all perfectly fine choices. Choosing an object that's "obvious" isn't an uncreative cop-out; it's proving to the rest of the group how much on the same page everyone is. Conversely, if someone's object does seem to be strange, resist the desire to negate it because it doesn't seem to "fit." So what if the "backyard" has a TV in it, or a rocket ship? It must belong in this specific, special backyard, since someone created it to go there!

The game is therefore also an opportunity to discuss how the details in an environment can tell us a lot about what specific kind of place it is, and what kinds of stories might happen there. A schoolroom with tiny kindergarten chairs and brightly-colored blocks is different from a schoolroom with big lab tables and test tubes, which is different from a schoolroom with inkwells and magic wands. If they all pay attention to those kinds of details as they arise, and build upon each other's ideas, they can work together to make a surprising, delightful, unique place to play.

Variations:

For very little children, mimed furniture is sometimes difficult to envision or keep consistent. In this case, you may want to use some real objects to stand in for imaginary ones, even if it's just to mark something's location using a chair or tape or fabric. This is something children often do anyway on their own, during independent creative play. Older children, though, can keep better track of invisible objects and it's usually better to use either all real furniture, or all imaginary, to open up possibilities for them.

Once you've built an environment, you can play around in it. Maybe everyone wants a turn walking through it by themselves. Perhaps everyone could take another turn, now that the environment is created, and explore it—possibly describing to the rest of the people something else they've discovered that lives in there… maybe the magical classroom has a jar of live frogs on the desk, and maybe someone's going to find it and let them all out.

Perhaps everyone wants to play in the environment together, as if they were all existing in that place at the same time. Perhaps a story will develop with everyone, or perhaps they will be content to explore and create self-directed activities independently, all at once.

Art: You could make the imaginary environment game into an art activity in a few different ways:

- You could have everyone create the imaginary place in space, and then you could have all the players individually draw a map or a picture of the space that the group created.
- Players could create an imaginary place on a smaller scale, using blocks, clay, or found objects; then everyone could draw a picture of the "real" things in that place that are represented by the other objects.
- Players could create an imaginary environment by taking turns adding to a map, rather than by creating it in space: each person could draw one piece on the map of a room. Players could create an imaginary building (or ship, or

castle) by each drawing a room on a floor plan. Or players could create an imaginary city or country, by adding elements to a map. (You could have one big drawing on a whiteboard, or you could pass pieces of paper around so that you end up with a host of different imaginary places.)

Writing: This environment exercise can even be used for creative writing: once a group has made a unique place (by any of the above methods), everyone can write a story that takes place in that environment, or a story in which that place is important.

MANDY KHOSHNEVISAN

Imaginary Activity ("Extras")

<u>For: Everyone</u>

group; physical; teamwork

Similar to creating an imaginary environment, players will create an invisible place, except this time they'll be portraying people instead of creating objects.

HOW TO PLAY:

Decide what kind of place you're going to create: this time, it will be a place where there might be a lot of people around (a fair, a circus, a sporting event, a park, a mall, etc), and declare that the space is now open. Players are now going to populate the space with "extras," as if they're background players in a movie. One by one, players add themselves to that imaginary location, using their bodies to show what their character is doing there. Once in the stage space, they should continue to occupy space, performing their activity and noticing the other people and things around them. The concept is similar to "I Am a Tree" (page 187), where players add themselves into a tableau based on what's there so far, except they can be moving instead of still.

For example, you might decide beforehand that the space is going to be a circus. Someone might go up and act like a clown. Someone else might enter and start juggling. A third person might choose to be a different kind of clown, working next to the first person. A fourth player might be a balloon seller. Five and six might be a parent and child, watching the juggler or the clowns. Everyone should add to the picture and be a moving, functioning part of the scene. When all the players have been added, you can set them "free" to interact and discover the circus.

Coaching Tips:

When adding to an environment, everyone should be doing *something*. It doesn't have to be a large, ostentatious movement, but everyone who's added something to the stage should be making a definitive choice to do a specific activity. For example, if your location is a mall, someone might choose to be sitting on a bench waiting for their friend. Though the act of "waiting" is not as dynamic as, say, playing on a play structure, it's still a choice, and distinctly different from "just sitting somewhere." Similarly, some activities may be very mobile (Mall Cop) while others may be very stationary (sitting in a massage chair). It takes both kinds to make a balanced, structured environment.

Variations:

Once everyone has added themselves to a scene, if you wish you can say "Action!" which will cause their voices to "turn on," so that they can interact with each other and have conversations. The circus performers can yell, "step right up," the small children can beg for candy or balloon animals; they can interact in a non-audience-focused way, as if they're just people behaving in a public space. When everyone is interacting as extras, no one's activity should "pull focus," meaning if a small child is begging for candy, the balloon seller should still be selling balloons to another group.

If you wish to eventually switch the focus of the game towards finding a shared activity, you can have everyone start out as extras, but then as soon as they see something happening that seems like fun, they can all join in (just like "Leave the Room for the Same Reason," page 102). The other characters should still keep the identity they've established previously: the clowns are still clowns, and the balloon seller is still selling balloons. They don't need to change the reality they've created, just the action happening within that reality. During this circus scenario, if a small child is begging its parent to buy candy, other players might decide that they want to get in line for cotton candy too, and the line starts getting longer and longer so that the child and the parent are at the very end. Or else everyone might want to beg that specific parent for candy too, so that eventually the lion tamer and the balloon seller and the clowns and everyone are on their knees, asking a small child's parent if they can have some candy.

MANAGED MISCHIEF — MAKING OFFERS WITH YOUR PHYSICALITY

Imaginary Sports

For: Basically everyone

group; physical; energy; teamwork; shared control

How to Play:

If your group is so inclined, you can play the previous game (**Imaginary Activity**) but designate your location/activity as a specific kind of game or sporting event. Then, when players enter one by one, they can locate themselves somewhere within the actual sporting event: players, referees, spectators, etc. When you call "Action," the players can even start reenacting that particular sport. In this case, it's like a mini-game but using an invisible ball. This is a great opportunity to challenge them to work together: can they play a real sport with an invisible ball or invisible equipment? And of course, because it's an invisible sport, it might start out as a "real" sport and change into something fun and wacky.

In order to do this, it's essential that they use their collective skills of "building the tower": they can self-narrate the sporting event, honoring the fact that whoever said it first was right. For example, an imaginary game of baseball could have a pitcher; a catcher; someone on first, second and third bases; and a batting lineup. There could be an announcer who describes the gameplay (essentially functioning as a narrator), or else players could narrate their own actions: "Awesome! I hit a home run!" Rather than argue, "No you didn't!" the players on the opposing "team" can embrace the Tug-o'-War spirit (page 222), and take this opportunity to be epically upset.

See how long you can play an imaginary sport with imaginary equipment, all working together to play the same game… because the secret of sporting fandom is that every game is a story: there are underdogs and villains; dramatic upsets and catastrophic mistakes; happy endings and sad ones. It's just as fun to play the euphoric winner as it is to lose catastrophically and get incredibly theatrically upset. Can the winners pour invisible Gatorade over each other? Can the losers fall down on the field and cry?

SHARING CONTROL

This basic skill is perhaps the most difficult to learn, and requires the most consistent sidecoaching to get players to change their habits. No one wants to "lose." But taking turns leading and following, winning and losing, is powerful self-confidence practice.

Tug o' War

<u>For: Everyone</u>

partners; physical

This is a quick exercise from Keith Johnstone, illustrating just how much we have to learn to share control.

How to Play:

You divide up everyone into partners, and have them pick up an imaginary ("space object") rope. Then you have a tug o' war! On 1, 2, 3, GO! each set of partners should tug and tug at the imaginary rope. What usually happens is that they will each pull and pull on that imaginary rope as it gets longer and longer… because everyone wants to win. You can watch this for a while, and then stop them and ask them to raise a hand if they won … it's probable that no one will do this. Then, you can illustrate a "real" tug o' war by having two kids grab hands and do it that way. Probably, it will be over very quickly.

Now, let them try again, and this time see if they can both agree to keep their rope the same length; practically, this means keeping their two sets of hands a uniform distance apart, and watching each other closely for pull and push movements. You might have them consciously practice just the pulling back and forth: when one partner gives a big tug and leans backward, the other should hang onto the "rope" and let it pull their body forward an equal amount. Then if they pull back again, their partner should follow suit, also pulled forward by the rope.

Once players are fairly comfortable with the mechanics of pulling back and forth, you can set them loose to practice on their own; challenge them to take turns losing at this imaginary tug-of-war.

Coaching Tips:

Challenging them specifically to *lose* emphasizes that it's OK if someone loses an imaginary tug-of-war, and also that it's pretty fun to lose spectacularly. Tumbling on the ground and being flung across the floor is pretty fun, after all. This principle applies more subtly when they're making up stories or playing pretend: if someone is playing the "bad guy," they are really, really not going to want to lose any battles or be defeated. If someone in a story is playing a trick on another character, that second character is likely going to invent reasons why they are not surprised and can't be fooled. You can have a conversation with them about villains and heroes and stories, and about what happens when no one loses. For a story to end, it means something has to change, and if no one crosses over to a different side, like getting pulled over the line in tug-o-war, the story can't end.

While experimenting with tug-of-war, some students may get clever and subversive, and start cutting the rope or letting go of it, or other things; they can experiment, as long as it's in the spirit of both partners experimenting with alternatives as a team. If one person is messing with the tug-of-war in order to make their partner look silly, or so they can get out of participating in the exercise, that's counter to our purposes. However, if *both* partners are interested in inventing absurd outcomes of the tug-of-war, by all means, encourage them!

Dolphin Training

For: Everyone

group; partners; physical; non verbal

Here's another exercise courtesy of Keith Johnstone, brought about because of the way training of real dolphins works. If the dolphin does something that approaches the desired trick, they get a treat. If the dolphin does something other than the trick, they get nothing. Based solely on positive feedback (how do you punish a dolphin?), the dolphin can learn to do a surprising array of things. We can also get our friends to do a surprising array of things, communicating only through rewards!

How to Play:

First:

You can play dolphin training with as few as two people, so it works well for partners; for a demonstration, it's best to start with one brave volunteer and the whole group as the trainers. The trainer(s) should secretly decide on a simple physical action that the first volunteer could easily perform. The "dolphin" shouldn't have any idea what the "trick" is, so during the selection process, you can have the volunteer leave the room, or just turn away and plug their ears (and probably hum), so they don't know what the action is. When all the trainers are clear on exactly what the action is, you can begin, setting the dolphin free in their environment. They can start out by simply existing in that environment: exploring the furniture, walking around, doing whatever they feel like. In the meantime, if they do something that seems like at least the beginning steps of the trick in question, give them their reward, which in this case is to say "ding!" (It's a little like playing Hot and Cold, without the Cold.) As the dolphin seeks out more rewards, trainers keep rewarding the behaviors that get closer and closer to the goal trick, until the dolphin performs the trick all by themselves.

For example, if their task is to sit on a specific chair, just walking towards the chair, or even just facing the chair instead of away from it, can earn them a "ding." Any other actions can be met with neutral silence. (We don't want to give them any "hints" ... with facial expressions, meaningful gazes, etc. Either it's a "ding" or it's absolutely no reaction at all.) For this example, now walking towards the chair might be the next step to earn them another "ding." Then, touching the chair — "ding!" Once they've stumbled onto the fact that the chair is the object of interest, there's only a limited scope of things they could do with it. They might pick it up and carry it somewhere; that would be met with silence. Putting it back down again might get a "ding," since we want it on the ground. When they finally do the trick, which is in this case sitting down in the chair, their reward is a glorious cascade of dings!

Second:

You might try another round in front of a group, just to make sure everyone's got it, and also to promote/reinforce the idea that it's light and fun, and that there should be no sounds for a "wrong" activity. Once the first person goes, and everyone experiences the delight of the exercise, you'll probably have a clamor of volunteers.

Let Them Loose:

When people seem to have gotten the gist, partner them up and let them take turns training each other. It's really fun to see this happen in one room, with everyone working at the same time. This is a game that most people find both fun and riveting; players tend to stay on task.

Coaching Tips:

As a facilitator, wander around and remind people not to talk except for "ding" ... the trainer shouldn't talk, and the "dolphin" shouldn't be talking directly to the trainer, though they may be making sounds if that's where their training is leading them. You should hear mostly a soundscape of dings... and likely giggling.

As far as "tricks," they can be as complicated as you wish. They don't have to be merely physical activities; you could train your "dolphin" to speak, sing, play any instruments in the room, and even play/sing a specific song, if it may be obvious what that song could be. The trick could also have multiple steps: Pick up that chair, move it over to the window, stand on it and look out and wave. Your group may get very complicated with their tricks, if they're really enjoying the game and want to work more on it.

Once they're on their own, there may be some groups that get a little stuck. There are a few common remedies. You can encourage the dolphins to explore more without waiting for the "ding"; often they get stuck because the trick is something that the dolphin just hasn't tried yet because they "don't know what to do." Encourage them to forget about the trainer for a little bit and just find ways to play in their space. (A conference with the trainer might give you some vague directional hints to drop.) Wiggle their bodies, make noise, play with things in the space, jump up and down... dolphins are playful creatures! (It's also fun and mischievous to play with your trainer a little bit by getting a ding, and then persisting in an activity that is fun but is clearly wrong and getting no dings whatsoever. In fact, it's even useful sometimes, to make sure that you're really on the right track.)

Variation (Advanced):

This is the subtle version: instead of "dings," the trainer can instead try to use super subtle facial and eye-contact cues to give approval and guide their subject through the trick. This should be conducted as if it were "clandestine," as if the trainer and the subject were trying not to have anyone else notice these "secret" nods and glances.

The Chair Game

For: Everyone

group; audience

There are those who play this game a different way, but I feel that way teaches kids to be argumentative and mean to each other. So I'm going to explain it this way instead.

How to Play:

There is one chair, with someone sitting in it. Everyone else lines up. In each turn, the player at the front of the line approaches the person in the chair with a reason that the person needs to get up. When the sitter leaves, the asker sits down, and it's the next person's turn.

The way I like to play this game, the person in the chair HAS to get up. This way, it's a taking-turns-with-control game. The person in the chair SEEMS to have the power, but the dynamic shifts abruptly when they react and leave. They should also overreact: what we might call "overaccepting" the offer. They don't need to preemptively get right up, but upon hearing what the stander has to say, they should overreact in a way that makes them vacate the chair. To give it some structure, I have the "stander" say three lines (comedy happens in threes, you know), each time expanding on their first offer, explaining more about why that offer, whatever it is, means that the person should vacate the chair. The sitter can "play dumb," or ask for more information, or be unconvinced—but after the third thing, they must make that their reason to leave.

Stander: I think you should get up.

Sitter: Why?

MANAGED MISCHIEF — SHARING CONTROL

> Stander: There's wet paint on that chair.
> Sitter: There is?
> Stander: Yep. I just finished painting it!
> Sitter: Oh no! My new pants! (stands up, checks pants, runs away; stander sits down)

It could be something about the chair, or something about the situation, that requires the sitter to get up. Players can make more fun discoveries if they approach the situation as characters, rather than just nebulous people. Often, students will focus on something about the chair itself, but you can guide them towards focusing on the situation. For example:

> Stander: Madam President, it's time.
> Sitter: Huh? Time?
> Stander: Yes! Everyone's waiting for you to give your speech!
> Sitter: My speech! I forgot all about it!
> Stander: You fell asleep! They've been waiting out there on the lawn for hours!
> Sitter: Oh no! Thank you for telling me! I must go at once!

Coaching Tips:

This is more satisfying if we remember our basic skills of being constructive rather than not constructive. If you guide the sitter to be confused and ask for clarification, the stander gets to elaborate on their situation and discover new things about it. If the sitter just says, "Nope!" then the stander doesn't have a lot to work with.

It might be like a little scene in which the "sitter" chooses to play a character that already knows about the activity: "Doctor, the patient is ready for you." "Ah yes, thank you." Or it might be Monty-Python-absurd to the point that the stander is actually tricking the sitter's character into believing an entire imagined reality, all in order to sit in the chair: "Doctor, the patient is ready for you." "Doctor? Am I a doctor?" "Of course! And the operation is right now!" "It is?" "Here's your scalpel!" "Thank you! Which way to the patient?"

Remembering to give our partner a good time, the stander's tactic should not be something that's going to make the other *actor* feel bad... "Get up! You're too ugly to sit there!" for example, could hurt some feelings. Or not — depending on the particular group dynamic. The group might all be good friends, and that actor might be really excited to agree to play a giant, drooling ogre, for example. But it's best to remind people to be kind to each other as actors; if something happens that makes me wonder, I usually ask the recipient, "Is/was that OK with you?" just to check in. And if they happily say, "Yup!" then we know.

What Comes Next

For: Ages 8 and up

(from Keith Johnstone)

partners, group

A lot of what Keith Johnstone is concerned with is getting people to work together and play nicely together: figuring out what to do to delight other people. What Comes Next is a good example of that, in both iterations. This is a game I learned at BATS Improv in San Francisco (and also from Keith himself).

How to Play:

As with Dolphin Training (page 224) there's a subject and an observer. It's easier to teach this exercise with one subject, and the rest of the group the audience. In the first iteration of this game, the subject is just the illustration of the story. The subject first asks, "What comes first?" The observer — in this case, someone from the rest of the audience group, might say anything — "You sit in a chair."

The subject does. "What comes next?"

Someone else suggests something. "You look out the window!"

The subject does. "What comes next?"

The idea is that the subject reenacts exactly what the audience says, without augmenting. They're like an instant storyboard, a computer game: a way for the audience to immediately see what they're creating. It's entirely possible that these stories will go wrong, or get weird; that's OK. And when it's the end, it'll "feel" like the end.

Once the group has mastered this skill as a whole audience, then you can break them up into partners or smaller groups to try playing it that way. (Sometimes three is a good number, so there's another person there to give ideas in case one person gets "stuck.") It's a good idea, as in any partnered exercise, to switch partners a few times.

The second iteration gives a little control back to the subject. In this version, the subject has the option to say, "Nope!" cheerfully in a happy voice if the suggestion doesn't "feel right." It's not a guessing game; the subject is not trying to make the guesser find the *exact* right thing. Instead, if the suggestion feels like it's something that should definitely come next, or if it seems like fun, then the subject will do it. But if it's something that feels out of place or icky, for whatever reason, then it's a "Nope!" There may be a string of "Nopes!" before the suggester hits upon something that feels right, and then, "What comes next?" again.

This is an exercise that teaches people more about each other, as individuals (one of the reasons I like it). The subject even has the power to "Nope!" the opening suggestion, so the suggester can think of a variety of scenarios in which to begin. Some people will be tickled to start out by flying a plane; others might prefer running through the jungle, or reading a book, or lying in bed. Some subjects will enjoy action; others intrigue. The goal is to make the person enjoy the process of experiencing their little story.

It's also sometimes easier to "think up" something to happen next if someone else has the power to say "Nope!" to it. It takes the pressure off the suggester, for having to think of the "perfect thing" to happen. I coach people that when they get stuck in this version of the game, to unstick themselves by rattling off a series of things that are really probably NOT going to be the right thing. (Sometimes it helps to play this game in a small group, so that one person is the subject and two or three or more people are there giving suggestions.)

Variations:

Writing: A small group of two or more people could use this exercise to write a story, or at least an outline for one — or perhaps the script for a graphic novel or screenplay for a film, since "what comes next" often contains a lot of action. Either the person asking, "what comes next?" could be the writer, with the other people offering suggestions, or else the person asking "what comes next?" could be onstage (or "onscreen") acting out their responses, while the rest of the group writes down the experience into a story or script.

Art: You could make this into a guided art project: the person asking "What comes next?" could be drawing a picture or making art in another medium. You could use the regular version, or incorporate the use of "Nope!"

Diamond Dance

<u>For: Everyone</u>

music, physical, dance, group

There are all sorts of ways to improvise choreography together; this is perhaps the simplest.

How to Play:

Divide into groups of four (if there's an odd number, having a few groups of three will also work). In each group, the four people stand in a diamond shape and all face the same direction, towards one of the points: if you think of them as the four points of the compass, everyone should start out facing north, for example. The person in front, who can't see any of the other people, is by definition the leader. They move, and the three others follow simultaneously, as in the Mirror exercise (page 182). The leader can transfer leadership at any time, merely by turning to face a different direction; because everyone else is following along, they will end up also facing that new direction, and a new person should be in the front — they're the new leader. I like to let them practice without music for a minute or two, making sure they cycle through all the leaders and making sure they have the hang of leading, following, and switching; then I'll switch on the tunes and let them go for it.

Coaching Tips:

If leaders seem stumped for something to do, I usually remind them, "It doesn't have to be interesting, it just has to be something!" Simplicity is key to this exercise. Movements don't need to be complicated to be impactful. One person raising both arms is a gesture; four people raising both arms is choreography! You also don't need to change movements as often as you think. Repeating the same move a minimum of four or eight times just ensures that the followers have time to really get the hang of it. And creating symmetry and pattern is always a good strategy. Just did something with your left hand? Try it with the right! Now the left again! Now the right!

Sometimes people are intimidated by the idea of "dance," and either attempt complex and difficult dance steps to show off their training, or else freeze entirely, stymied by lack thereof. But it just needs to be movement; it doesn't have to be "dance." I worked with a class of young teenagers once where one young gentleman was too cool to "dance" and quietly developed his own schtick. He would follow the others' dance steps, but whenever it was his turn to lead, he would instead mime everyday activities. Four kids grooving to the music while brushing their teeth and fishing, in unison, had us rolling on the floor with laughter.

Variations:

To provide helpful restrictions, you might challenge them to do a specific kind of dance or movement. A dance could start with an idea from the audience, and you could challenge players to observe each other and echo or respond when it's their turn to lead. It could be a dance-related suggestion: "This dance is a ballet." It could be a style inspired by non-dance movement: "This dance is about chickens." Or, you could give them something more emotional and abstract: "This dance is about winter."

The diamond (or triangle) formation is just the tip of the iceberg, when it comes to ways to lead and follow in groups. Once they've gotten the hang of it, if this is a fun exercise that they enjoy, you can think up all kinds of formations and ways to dance together. Have people take turns leading a whole crowd! Try dancing in a circle while all watching each other! Have everyone choose a partner and have everyone play the "mirror" game while dancing! The possibilities are only limited to your own imagination.

(We totally used to diamond dance at parties in college. For real. I've done it at improvisor weddings. And I've seen my middle school students do it at parties too. Nothing will make you feel more included at an awkward dance-type situation than to be able to have some ridiculous fun dancing in unison with your friends.)

Give and Take

<u>For: Everyone</u>

groups; shared control; music; dance

This is a movement exercise that is also fun to do to music. It's a different way to make something look choreographed, but it's more freeform. It's also a great physical illustration of the give and take between collaborators on basically any project.

How to Play:

You can play with everyone all at once if you like, though this exercise also benefits from smaller groups that can watch each other. The players spread through the space; maybe they start in a fun tableau with everyone in their own pose, or maybe they just find a place to be. They should arrange themselves in a starting pose that's easy to stay frozen in: standing with one leg over your head may be fancy, but it's a position that's hard to hold. Before we begin, I tell them, "Everyone in this game is either moving, or not moving. The only thing that counts as not moving, is not moving. Scratching your head is moving. Looking around to see who else is moving, is moving. You should be completely, totally frozen, otherwise you're the one moving."

When everyone has found their starting place, I tell them, "Okay, exactly one person has to be moving at all times, and everyone else should be frozen!" and then I give them the signal to begin. (If I'm using music, that signal would be the music starting. I find it's often easier to play music, since it gives them some context and encouragement to move. But you don't have to.) At this point, one person will start to move. Who?

Well, the person who starts to move first is the person who moves first. It's one of those "group mind" things. If this is really freaking them out, or if the group is very young, it's OK to designate ahead of time the person who's going to move first, when the piece begins. They might need that much direction, in the first couple of rounds.

The "rule" in the beginning is that exactly one person must be moving at all times — but that doesn't mean it's the SAME person. And how do you switch between who moves? This is a silent game, so there should be no verbal communication. There are two basic ways to pass the torch, so to speak: the person moving can stop, prompting someone else to pick up the movement (ie, *giving* the movement); or someone else can start moving, prompting the first person to stop (ie, *taking* the movement). If two people start moving at once, there's a brief nonverbal negotiation, and one of them will probably stop.

During the round, let them keep just one person moving, for a while. After perhaps a minute or so, when they've gotten the hang of it, go ahead and call out that now TWO people should be moving at all times. This works much the same way, except that everyone's peripheral perception needs to be expanded just a little bit more. When they've gotten the hang of two, you can add a third person, a fourth, everyone-but-one, then everyone dancing together, and then have them find an ending together: when everyone is frozen, that's the end!

Coaching Tips:

As outlined above, anything that's not stillness is "movement." I usually use the word "movement" instead of "dancing," because players will often be scared off by the idea of having to come up with dance moves. Walking, running, creeping like a creature, and yes, dancing, all count as continuing the movement. A caveat is just that if someone's chosen movement is small or close to the body, the other players might not be able to see what's happening—so you can encourage players to commit to large movements, in order to help each other out. When in doubt, just walk.

In the first few rounds, players are likely to feel they need to "send" the movement to a specific person, possibly by freezing right next to someone, or else by making a specific "sending" gesture in their direction where they can see it. Sometimes this works, and the indicated person accepts the impulse and starts moving. Sometimes it doesn't work as intended, and no one starts moving, or someone *else* picks it up. But none of this matters; the only important thing is that *someone* keep the ball in the air, figuratively, by making sure that one person is moving at all times. As they progress, you can challenge them to become bolder, and transfer the movement just by stopping, or to be bold by taking the movement; see if they can pass it around faster and faster.

Variations:

Depending on the group and their interest, you can use this basic format to play in lots of different ways.

You could try it without verbal cues, to see if they can transition from one person moving, to two, to three, etc., and then finding an ending, all organically without outside directions. (My high school students used to do this as an opening to their improv shows; when it flows organically, it looks even more like magic.)

You might try playing with adding more parameters to the piece, in terms of theme, structure, or quality of movement. For example, you might challenge players to notice the way that others are moving, and repeat either their direct movements or style of travelling. (Long lyrical arms; stomping and clapping; running in circles; moving like animals… anything they see someone else doing that looks like fun.)

You could also declare ahead of time, before the piece starts, a quality of movement to play with, "Opposites"-style (see page 205). You could have them all think about the same style: "For this round, we're all going to move heavily," for example, and see all the different interpretations of that way of moving. Or else, you could pick two opposites: "We're all either going to move fast, or slow!" Or, "We're all going to move either happily, or sadly!" You could decide on a more concrete theme: We're all cats! or, We're all animals! Or, you could pick an abstract theme: This will be a piece about snow! or weather! or the last day of school! This may well inspire a very broad range of interpretations: everything from jumping for joy, to shining like the sun, to tossing imaginary hats in the air…

Sheep ünd Wolf

<u>For: Everyone</u>

group, nonverbal, physical

I believe this game was made up by two of my Improv 103 TAs in college: Dave McGee and Matt Olsen. They invented it as a way to warm up while working on status switches. It's the best tag game: fun, organized, and just ever so slightly dangerous. I've never had anyone hurt themselves while playing it, but you never know. Also, did I mention it's really fun? And that it was invented by adults who enjoyed playing it, themselves?

How to Play:

Here's how it works: everyone is scattered around crouched on the ground; they are rocks. There are two people standing: one sheep, ünd one wolf. The wolf (who growls like a wolf) chases the sheep (who baaaas like a sheep) around the field. If the wolf tags the sheep, the sheep becomes the *new* wolf with a loud roar, and the erstwhile wolf becomes the sheep with a frightened baaaa. BUT, if the sheep can hide behind/next to a rock before being tagged, the sheep now becomes that rock, the rock rears up and becomes the new wolf with a roar, and the wolf — who had been the chaser — becomes the sheep, and must flee. This is amazingly a fast-paced game that is still pretty organized, since there should only be two people running at any one time.

Coaching Tips:

Just like with real status switches, players will figure out pretty soon that what makes the game fun is the sudden and drastic shifts. If the sheep just runs and runs and stays far out of range of the wolf, give a time limit, or impose a space restriction, or do something else to suggest that the switches happen more quickly. The terrifying/delightful moments when someone gets tagged, or the sheep hides behind a rock, or when everyone at once forgets what to do next, are the best moments of the game.

MAKING OFFERS WITH YOUR STORIES

14

For older or more advanced students, or those interested in stories, improvisational techniques can be great for spurring creative writing. Most of the games in the book can be played by everyone ages three or four and up, but some of these writing and storytelling games are more successful with a basic grasp of literacy and verbal fluency. Many of these games can be played either verbally or in writing, or in combination ... I urge you to use your imagination!

Story Spine

<u>For: Age 7 and up</u>
circle; group; partners; quiet time

Writing teachers use several different terminologies to teach and describe story structure, using different levels of vocabulary: from "Beginning - Middle - End" to "Exposition - Rising Action - Climax - Falling Action - Denouement." These are great terms for analyzing existing stories—but Story Spine is a great way to think about stories while you're right in the middle of them. Kenn Adams, who created many useful tools for improvisors and storytellers, developed a structure that he dubbed the Story Spine.[1] Since its development, it's been used by improvisors around the world. It goes:

Once upon a time...
And every day...
Until one day...
Because of that...
Because of that...
Because of that...
Until finally...
And ever since then....
(optional: The moral of the story is...)

As you can see, it generally follows the same shape as the more "official" literary descriptions of a story structure. The great thing about

---
[1] Kenn Adams has many excellent books about improvising and stories... check them out!

MANAGED MISCHIEF — MAKING OFFERS WITH YOUR STORIES

the Story Spine is that you can use the steps of it to build a story, using the steps in their own words!

How to Play:

You can have your group of players tell a story one line at a time, each taking one step of the Story Spine. It's most effective to go in a circle first, so that everyone can hear the same story, all at once. (If you need more "because of that"s, you can add them until it feels like the right time for "Until finally.")

Here's a very, very basic example I just made up:

Once upon a time... there was a little girl.

And every day... she went outside to water the flowers.

Until one day... she found that her flowers had all been eaten!

Because of that... she looked closer and found some footprints in the dirt.

Because of that... she followed the footprints, where they led all the way to a rabbit hole.

Because of that... she concluded that a rabbit had eaten her flowers!

Because of that... she said loudly into the rabbit hole, "You rabbit! Did you eat my flowers? You better say you're sorry!"

Until finally... the rabbit came out and was very apologetic, and promised never to do it again, and invited her in for a cup of tea.

And ever since then... the little girl had lovely flowers AND a rabbit friend.

The moral of the story is... sometimes persistence pays off.

It's a good idea to go around quite a few times the first time; there are sometimes some kinks that need working through, in order for everyone to "get it." When players get the hang of it, you can break them up into smaller groups or partners and let them use the Story Spine that way.

Coaching Tips:

There are some common things that happen in the discovery of this game, which can usually be ironed out by paying attention to our basic concepts: see what's happening, help it happen. Sometimes we get a little lost when we haven't been listening, or haven't made sure that the steps of the Story Spine really follow one from the other. For example, the "Because of that" should really be something that was *directly caused* by the previous step, not just "something else that happened." Sometimes this not-listening occurs because we're thinking so hard about the great thing that we want to add to the story, that we didn't pay attention to what was actually happening, and now our contribution no longer makes sense.

Sometimes, we get carried away with events of the story, and forget the person, place or thing that the events are happening *to:* whoever (or whatever) was featured in the "Once upon a time." Young storytellers occasionally need reminders that stories usually happen to main characters; as a story is progressing, you can sidecoach them to mention how the events are affecting the main character.

Plus, as I described in "Word-at-a-time Story" (page 114), you might very well get, once upon a time there was a guy, and every day he went fishing, "Until one day he died!" The impulse here is one of mischief, because it's very likely that they're trying to mess with the story. (If you want, though, sure, why not? You can follow through: what happens NEXT, after he dies? This unexpected twist might create a fascinating, surprising, weird and magical story!)

MANAGED MISCHIEF — MAKING OFFERS WITH MANDY

Variations:

You can use the Story Spine in all sorts of situ⸱ creating stories by directly following the steps, or u that already exist. You can also add a higher amoun⸱ on each step of the story, instead of just one sentence per step. ⸱ is a good way to illustrate how story-creators (authors, playwrights, etc) can add lots of details to their story, but still keep to an understandable structure in order to keep the story moving.

Sentence-at-a-time story: With older students, you might try to tell a story one sentence at a time, but without necessitating that each sentence be the next step on the Story Spine. In this case, the storytelling players can hold the structure in their minds, keeping track of what step they're on. You might even try staying on one step all the way around the circle, before progressing to the next step, in order to practice adding detail:

A: *Once upon a time*, there was a guy named Jason.
B: He was very tall and strong.
C: The people in his village whispered that he could lift an entire cow.
D: He had black hair that came down to his knees.
E: He had only one room in his house.
F: He had a pet goat who lived in his house with him.
A: *And every day*, he took his pet goat for a walk in the hills.
B: His job was to wander through the hills looking for bad guys.
C: When he went, he took a big walking stick with him, which was the size of a tree.
D: If there were ever any bad guys around, he chased them away, waving the stick.

E: His goat also chased them, baaaaaa-ing like crazy.

F: Whenever they chased away a bad guy, they always stopped at the river and took a swim to cool off and also celebrate.

A: *Until one day…* etc.

(This is a great preparatory exercise for **Color/Advance**, below.)

Onstage: You can have a narrator or a few narrators tell a Story Spine or sentence-at-a-time story, one step at a time, while the rest of the group acts it out. (This is a great way to cement the fact that it works much better when it's about a main character, since everyone can actually *see* who the story is about and watch them enact it.)

Writing: You can do line-at-a-time stories on paper; just pass the papers around the circle or back and forth. Writers can either follow the Story Spine with each step, or just keep it in their minds as they write one sentence at a time. (As with all collaborative writing, remind them to read the whole story so far before adding a sentence.)

Art: This exercise would lead nicely into the concepts of storyboarding or comics/graphic novel writing: by identifying the building blocks of storytelling, it makes it more clear for budding artists exactly what pictures might be important to include. You might have the students illustrate an existing story or book, by drawing the events that fulfill the steps of the Story Spine. Or perhaps they make up their own wordless story, drawing just eight pictures, one for each step. You might even experiment with a picture-at-a-time story: each student draws the first panel, the "Once upon a time…" and then passes it around, each person drawing the next picture on someone else's comic strip, and so on around the group.

Dance: Since a ballet tells a story through movement, you might try having students create ballets, one Story Spine step at a time. You could have a narrator switch steps, saying, "Once upon a time:" and then the dancers presenting, wordlessly, the contents of that step. When the narrator says, "And every day:" the dancers move to the second step, showing what happens every day in the world set up by their first step… and so on. Since it's ballet, it could be as concrete or as abstract as you like, and I bet the feeling of a story arc will still make emotional sense to the audience.

.nce

For ~~age~~ 8 and up

partners; group; writing; quiet time

This is a versatile exercise, which you can employ in several media to explore adding detail to your stories, and also to practice the difference between adding more information to the story, and actually moving the *plot* forward. By playing and listening to *when* the caller switches between color and advance, storytellers can also develop their sense of what the audience/reader may want to hear more about (and therefore also what they don't).

HOW TO PLAY:

This works best in partners or groups of three; for a big group, you may want to have a pair demonstrate for the group first before sending players off to work on their own. One person is the storyteller, and one person is going to act as the "director," calling either "Color," or "Advance" as the storyteller speaks. Depending on which mode they're in, the storyteller should try to provide *only* that type of information, though in practice these modes are often combined. My metaphor for color and advance is a leaf floating down a river: the river advances on and on in a definite path, but every now and then, the water might sweep the leaf off to the side in an eddy, creating a little whirlpool, exploring the bank, before moving on down the river to its destination.

"Advance" mode should be simply action: what happens next, and next, and next, and next. This mode often sounds Hemingwayesque, and for the purposes of *this exercise* should be devoid of description. "Sally opened her front door. She looked around to see if there was anyone waiting for her. No one was there. She grabbed her backpack and walked down the street to the park on the corner."

"Color" mode is when the plot should stop moving forward because the storyteller is describing or elaborating the moment. It's a way to expand and explore that frozen moment in time for a little while, because there's more information that the reader/audience needs to know before continuing the action. The color could be concrete: things the reader might perceive with their five senses in that frozen moment of story time. "The sun shone in the park and warmed the bench; the air smelled like cut grass and lawnmower fumes." It could be emotional or internal: what the people in the story are feeling in that moment. "Sally was shaking with fear, and her breath got faster and faster." It could be memory or backstory: context from past events that influences or helps explain something in the present moment. "She remembered: last time they mowed the grass in this park, the lawnmower went crazy and ran away! Sally wondered whether it was still living in that secret cave under the footbridge."

As in that example, the color added to a story can often influence the action, as you add details you never even thought to think of. In writing that example, I had no idea that there would be a lawnmower monster — or even, frankly, that the examples would be connected.

In partners, the storyteller speaks, while the director can say "color" or "advance" at any time. When the director calls for "color," they can elaborate, depending on what they want to hear more about: "Color the lawnmower monster!" (You can even begin the story with a directive of either "color" or "advance"; the story as told might start anywhere: action, atmosphere, object, location… have fun with it!)

The story is over either when the storyteller comes to a natural end, or else when you've decided time is up and call out, "Find an ending!" If you're working in partners, they can switch roles and try again.

Coaching Tips:

Remind storytellers to keep the stories about a main character, if possible, and not to think too hard about what to say. If storytellers are stuck, the directors can be more specific in their requests for color.

Also remind storytellers that "advance" should have virtually no descriptions, and "color" should *not* move the story forward. They're probably well-trained to mix the two concepts, especially if they're already avid readers or writers — but the purpose of the exercise is to help players sort out the difference between the two concepts, and to notice how and when to consciously and judiciously switch modes. The director functions as the audience, telling the storyteller what they want to hear more of, in order for the story to feel more satisfying.

There are also "games" to be found here, as in any exercise. Directors might make the storytellers color or advance for long stretches of time, or use "color" to drill down farther on a specific path: "In the corner there was a desk." "Color the desk." "It's a wooden desk; um, it was carved in England in 1725 by Steven Smith." "Color Steven Smith!" "Steven Smith was a poor woodworker…" etc etc. The purpose of this exercise is as much or more in the journey as it is in the destination: it doesn't so much matter whether you create a "successful" story, as it is to explore the dynamics and the balance between color and advance, and to surprise and delight yourself by saying things you hadn't thought of.

MANAGED MISCHIEF — MAKING OFFERS WITH YOUR STORIES

Variations:

This technique, set free to wander where it will, is great for telling fantastical, made-up stories that usually surprise the teller. You might use the technique in more focused activities, to work on different aspects of writing:

Genre: You could give storytellers a specific genre to work in, like fairy tale or scary story or adventure story… it's a great way to explore the tropes of a genre, and how the specific language of the narration, and the events of the plot, signal to the reader/listener what genre the story is in. Conversely, you could have the students begin the story in "color" mode, describing a location or an object; depending on what kind of setting emerges from the description, it might suggest a genre to the storyteller, and then that in turn would influence the rest of the story. A description of a haunted house might end up being a scary story about monsters, an adventure story about kids finding treasure, or even a silly story about a friendly ghost; each of these scenarios suggests a category of characters and events.

Monologue: You could use the technique to listen to a first-person story or anecdote told by a made-up character. Storytellers could develop the character as the story goes along, listening to what kind of person must be telling this story, or else create the character ahead of time.

Memoir/True Story: You could have storytellers recount something that happened to them in real life, with the "directors" asking them for details and clarification with "color," just like a made-up story. It's a great technique for making people realize that telling a true story benefits just as much from story structure and key details as a made-up story does.

Quiet Time: You can also play Color/Advance with writing: have everyone writing their own story or monologue, and every now and then have the facilitator call out either "Color" or "Advance"; writers should immediately transition into the mode that was called out, and remain in that mode until the director switches. Since the directions won't be based on anyone's specific story timing, it's good practice for the writers, incorporating these arbitrary direction-changes into their own story and challenging themselves to make the switches make sense. Again, the goal is that hopefully writers will surprise themselves.

Writers can even play Color/Advance all alone! I've done it for writing practice before. You can set a timer to go off at either regular intervals, or random ones (I found a smartphone app that functions as a game timer; it's got a customizable "random" setting). Decide on a mode to start writing in, and then switch modes every time the timer goes off.

Art: To try Color/Advance as an art activity, you could have an artist work on a drawing or painting. It could be a drawing of a specific, concrete image (an imaginary portrait, an animal, a place, a still life, etc), or else an abstract work. Their director would call out color/advance, which in this case could mean either "coloring" by working on increased detail in one part of their artwork (or indeed adding literal color), or else "advancing" by adding lines, shapes, and forms elsewhere in the piece. Just like above, everyone could have a director personally observing, who adds detail like, "Color the hair!" or you could have a facilitator arbitrarily calling it for a whole group at once—or set a timer and try it by yourself!

Fortunately/Unfortunately

<u>For: Age 7 and up</u>

groups, partners, onstage, circle

Another way to look at the mechanics of stories, besides the linear progression of the Story Spine, is the way in which the main character is often put through a series of trials — and doesn't necessarily navigate successfully through them. If the hero wins every battle, there's no suspense. We have to believe that the hero's in legitimate danger of losing, sometimes. But it's difficult for younger children to write a story where they (or their hero) loses (see the section on Shared Control and Tug o' War, page 222). This game makes it fun to get the main character into trouble and then out again.

How to Play:

Designate two narrators: one for Fortunately, and one for Unfortunately. You can also select three or four actors to act out the story. In this game, the narrators give the information, and the actors act out each step of the story. They can act it out in mime and sound effects; they don't need to use dialogue if it's not necessary.

The Fortunately narrator goes first: they set out the characters of the story, and then give the first action. The Unfortunately narrator then gives an unfortunate consequence of that action:

> A: Once upon a time, there was a queen who had three daughters who lived in a palace on a hill. One day, they all went for a walk.

B: Unfortunately, they managed to lock themselves out of the palace.

A: Fortunately, they had hidden a spare key under a rock at the bottom of the moat.

B: Unfortunately, the key was gone!

The game continues until the story reaches a place that feels like the end (you may have to help it along).

Coaching Tips:

The narrators might find themselves in a contest of using the fortunately/unfortunately to cancel out the events in the story. The "unfortunately" step can feel very close to the idea of knocking down the tower. See if you can guide them to make each step advance the plot and get the main characters farther into trouble. I've definitely had multiple classes of students do some version of this story:

A: Once upon a time, there were two princesses who lived in a castle together.

B: Unfortunately, they were attacked by a dragon and they died.

A: Fortunately, they came back to life, and captured the dragon!

B: Unfortunately, the dragon got free and killed them all again.

And so on. As you can see, these two fictitious narrators are basically fighting amongst themselves for dominance of the story. One's offer cancels the information given in the previous offer. There's a small but subtle difference between an unfortunate event that stops the action and one that advances the story. If the players work together instead of directly cancelling each other, they can still both have much of what they want:

> A: Once upon a time, there were two princesses who lived in a castle together.
> B: Unfortunately, they were attacked by a dragon!
> A: Fortunately, they managed to capture the dragon!
> B: Unfortunately, the dragon got free and captured THEM!
> A: Fortunately, the dragon decided not to eat them.
> B: Unfortunately, the dragon decided to eat them LATER, so he took them back to his nest!

This story has more of a probability of progressing. Our protagonists are in danger, and that danger will take them through the twists and turns of an adventure, without immediately ending the story.

That's Better!/That's Worse!

<u>For: Age 7 and up</u>

groups; circle; partners

This game plays with the same ideas as Fortunately/Unfortunately, but with more room to explore building up high stakes for a character.

How to Play:

In a circle, we start a story, one line at a time. The once-upon-a-time-and-every-day parts are fairly neutral. After setting up the basic situation, every sentence after that should either make the situation better for the main character, or worse. The whole circle will then either chant, "That's better!" or "That's worse!" depending on which it is. The story proceeds like that, with each subsequent person adding a sentence, followed by the group, proclaiming, "That's better!" or "That's worse!" You have a little more freedom than in the previous game, since you don't have to directly alternate between Fortunately and Unfortunately. (I think we may have developed this game at the Un-Scripted Theater Company, in order to practice having things happen that were actively either better or worse for the protagonist, rather than just "something else happening.")

A: Once upon a time, there was a princess who wanted to be a hero.

B: Every day, she went out in the yard and practiced with her sword.

C: She got really, really good at swordfighting.

All: "That's better!"

D: One day, the castle was invaded by the neighboring king!

All: "That's worse!"

E: The soldiers swept through the castle and surrounded the princess!

All: "That's worse!"

F: The princess tried to fight back with her swordfighting skills.

All: "That's better!"

G: But there were too many guys to fight against, and so they took her prisoner.

All: "That's worse!"

(et cetera)

Keep on around the circle, until the story ends (or until you find the need to stop). It might be a happy ending, or an unfortunate one!

Coaching Tips:

Players don't need to directly alternate between better and worse; the protagonist might go quite a long streak in a row of events happening for the better — or for the worse. It's fun to see just how the tension builds on a long streak of either really good things, or really bad things. How much better can things get? How much worse? This game demonstrates that a wild roller coaster ride of ups and downs can be much more satisfying, narratively speaking, than a gentle, obvious coast to the finish line.

String of Pearls

<u>For: Age 8 and up</u>
groups; audience

This fascinating and often absurd game is about stringing sentences together into a story, making everyone's sentences make sense together by hook or by crook. Playing the game requires many different skills all at once: listening to each other, remembering your own input, tracking a story, and helping all the available pieces fit together.

HOW TO PLAY:

String of Pearls has players create a story one sentence at a time — but not in order! The story takes place along a horizontal line onstage, like a story timeline. To begin, one person takes a place in the line and says one sentence. Right now the story consists of just that one sentence. Let's say,

A: The sun shone high overhead.

It doesn't need to mean anything in particular, yet; it's only one sentence!

The next player's job is to add another sentence, choosing both what the sentence is, and where in the story it should go. So, they walk up to the stage and first place their body along the story timeline, so that we can see what this new sentence's relationship is to the rest of the story (in this case, just one sentence). For western writing systems, the story timeline reads left to right as we look at it from the audience, so if the second sentence goes *before* the first one in the story, the second player should stand to the audience's left of the other, and vice versa. Then, the

MANAGED MISCHIEF — MAKING OFFERS WITH YOUR STORIES

players read the story to us in order, starting from our left to right, with each player exactly repeating their sentence as they originally said it:

B: Priscilla wanted to be an astronaut.

A: The sun shone high overhead.

With just two sentences, the story still doesn't make any sense, and that's OK. A third player now adds their body and their voice to the story, and they read it again:

B: Priscilla wanted to be an astronaut.

A: The sun shone high overhead.

C: The cat was worried.

One by one, players add sentences to the story, trying to tie the existing parts together into a coherent whole:

B: Priscilla wanted to be an astronaut.

D: She walked into the backyard where her homemade spaceship was.

A: The sun shone high overhead.

C: The cat was worried.

B: Priscilla wanted to be an astronaut.

D: She walked into the backyard where her homemade spaceship was.

E: The cat was sleeping on top of it.

A: The sun shone high overhead.

C: The cat was worried.

B: Priscilla wanted to be an astronaut.

D: She walked into the backyard where her homemade spaceship was.

E: The cat was sleeping on top of it.
A: The sun shone high overhead.
C: The cat was worried.
F: The engine started right up!

As the game progresses, you see how the sentences are strung together, and the story becomes more and more coherent until you find what feels like a complete piece (or you run out of people).

Coaching Tips:

The first few sentences can feel like a giant leap into the unknown, and that's all right. Again, we don't have to hem and haw about coming up with the "best sentence"; any sentence will fit into the story just fine, since the story hasn't even been created yet! In fact, it's often even easier, or at least more magical, if the first two sentences sound completely unrelated. That way, other players can just see what's happening, and fill in what to them might be "obvious" connections between the two ideas. Connections often feel easier, since you aren't so much "inventing" as just using your powers of observation to fill in what you see in the space between.

If your players need a boost with this game, you could try it with the first two people adding the first and last sentences of the story (in either order). This ensures that the first two sentences will be far enough apart that the other players can fill in the spaces between them. This takes out some creative possibilities, but may be easier at least to start with.

How long is a story? When starting, it's helpful to limit the story to a selected number of players, and let each player have one sentence. You can select a group of players to come up and wait in the wings; usually five to seven is a good number. That way, they know they're playing from the very beginning of the story (as opposed to having a set number of players come up from the audience), so they have agreed to the responsibility to complete the story and will already be paying attention and thinking about how to make connections.

Only add one sentence to the story at a time, and each time you add a sentence, the whole story must be read aloud from left to right. This reinforces how each new sentence affects the narrative so far, and the repetitive rhythm is rather pleasing, as each person settles into their job of repeating their sentence.

The task of the later players is more difficult, since as the number of remaining players decreases, the number of sentences left in which to tie up the story likewise decreases. Narrowing of possibilities, however, is often a springboard for creativity. What one sentence can we come up with that will bridge the seemingly unfathomable chasm between the sentences on either side? It's these times when you can surprise yourself. (And if it doesn't entirely "make sense?" So what! You tried, and probably made yourself laugh by trying.)

Variations:

Endpoints: A good way to begin playing this game is to have the first two players create the endpoints of the story: between the two of them, in either order, they'll establish the first line and the last line. Then their fellow players can just fill in the rest. Once your group feels they've conquered this version, you can move on to playing it more free-form.

The Chair Version: To work a different sort of muscle, you can establish seven story spots, and challenge players to add sentences only where there's an empty slot. Set out three chairs (or other objects) evenly spaced, so that the seven spots are the three chairs, the spaces between them, and one space on either side. It's sneaky because seven steps is how many there are in the Story Spine (page 244), so you could even play those two games together! And if you're feeling frisky, you can add more chairs to add more spaces.

No Limits: For those more advanced, or for smaller groups of players, you can try a version where players can add more than one sentence: once everyone's added one sentence, if the story's not done, you can still keep going until it feels finished. To add a second sentence, an onstage player can sprint to a different place in the string; now that person has two places to keep track of, and must move between them each time the story's read out loud. The group can keep adding sentences until the story feels finished. The added challenge of sprinting back and forth, and remembering where you were, makes this an especially funny and energetic version. Even a group of two or three people can play the game this way — especially if they use the chair system to keep track of where all the spots are.

EPILOGUE

Congratulations! If you're reading this, you've either read through all of the previous chapters, or else accidentally turned to this page.

In either case: the previous chapters represent a toolkit — or perhaps a starter kit. Once you've read the info and the games, you'll try some of them out. In trying them out, you may have ideas about how to modify them to fit your needs. You or your players may come up with great ideas about where and when and how to play these games, that nobody has thought of before. That's great! I want this book and these games to be a springboard for creativity, not just the definition of creativity. Jump off this book to reach discoveries of your own! (Depending on how thick it is, you may need to use several copies.) There are also plenty of other games and variations out there. Using the skills and direction in this book, you can try out other games, or make up your own!

Maybe you've played through all of these games and incorporated them into your daily life. Or maybe, there's just only one, just one, that you and your family or classroom really really love. Maybe you play it every day, and make up new ways to play it, and have your toys play it and make your friends play it and create an ongoing story where the characters play it. I would love that! Use the tools that speak to you in the moment, and come back for the other ones when you're looking for something new. I've played these games for years and years, and I definitely go through phases where one way of working makes a lot of sense to me suddenly.

May the spirit of improv spread joy, delight, and creativity insidiously through your life. Enjoy!

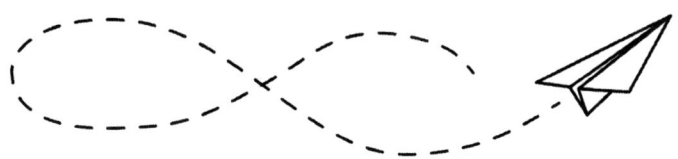

APPENDICES

APPENDIX THE FIRST

The Advanced Concept That Will Blow Your Mind
or,
What We Talk About When We Talk About Status

I've mentioned the concept of status several times above, but I chose not to delve into it until this section of the book. It's a whole different way to see the world, and once you start, it's difficult to stop. This is big-picture stuff. If you decide to work discussions about status into your formal or informal improv sessions, it may well give you a new way to think about and understand behavior: from what characters do in works of literature, to how people present their own images to the world. It even helps explain and explore common kid-behavior situations such as shyness and bullying.

When I began studying improv, one of the most game-changing concepts for me was the idea of status. Keith Johnstone talks about status in his book *Impro*,[1] and for me at least, the concept of status is one of the most openly secret ways of describing and analyzing human behavior that I've come across so far. Basically, it describes and makes apparent the ways in which we're all constantly affecting each other in everyday life. Every interaction between two people is a status interaction. The crazy thing is, we all kind of know this already — we know what it feels like,

---

1 There's a whole chapter about it... pp. 33-74.

we can recognize it when it happens, BUT we don't really have words to describe it in layperson vocabulary. (Not even actors always study status in detail; it appears to be the provenance of the improvisor.) Once there's a common vocabulary to describe the contents of these interactions, you find yourself seeing it everywhere. It's the ultimate level of "seeing what's happening."

In regular-people life, we tend to use the word "status" to describe someone's social, professional, or economic standing: conventional wisdom defines a high-status person as a rich guy or a president or a super-popular kid. This may indeed be how we figure out how we think we should treat people, but personal status in the improv sense is much more granular than that, more moment-to-moment, and it has to do with the interaction itself, and with the way that people behave towards each other. Verbal and non-verbal cues intersect.

We describe similar status-based interactions among animals, and use some of that vocabulary metaphorically to refer to people: describing someone as an "alpha male," for example. But we don't tend to think about status in everyday interactions among regular humans, although it's absolutely the same thing, and absolutely pervasive. Coaches, psychologists, and self-help gurus talk about reading and harnessing the power of body language, and that's also part of talking about status. There are people whose natural or adopted status measures happen to work in their favor, and there are people for whom their daily presentation works against them. Because we have no vocabulary to speak about it or analyze it, we are often helpless against these tendencies. But once we have those tools, we have the power to see more of what's happening, and we also have the power to help ourselves help it happen, in a way that works in our favor. We can analyze and then *change* the way we present ourselves and interact with others, both onstage and in real life, to help ourselves.

Keith Johnstone writes about the moment he became aware of this concept, while he was trying to figure out why he'd been having no luck getting his actors to replicate conversations that actually felt normal and real:

> "'Try to get your status just a little or just above your partner's,' I said, and I insisted that the gap should be minimal. The actors seemed to know exactly what I meant and the work was transformed. The scenes became 'authentic,' and actors seemed marvellously observant. Suddenly we understood that every inflection and movement implies a status, and that no action is due to chance, or really 'motiveless.' It was hysterically funny, but at the same time very alarming. All our secret manoeuvrings were exposed."[2]

Somehow our brains automatically slide over status transactions, noticing their effects but neglecting to tell us about them directly. It's as if there's a great unspoken gentleman's agreement to overlook the motivations behind everyone's behavior. Johnstone concludes, "Normally we are 'forbidden' to see status transactions except when there's a conflict. In reality status transactions continue all the time."[3]

Status behavior is something that we observe all the time ... so when you play the status games below (all from Keith Johnstone or based on his work) and start consciously thinking about it, players often find it easy to draw useful conclusions from a small amount of prodding. The "status thing" makes sense, once you call attention to it.

Talking about status is probably something that should be done in a more structured environment with a facilitator, and it's probably also not for kids younger than age 8 or 9 (although your results may vary). The

---

2   *Impro*, p. 33
3   ibid.

following exercises are more like acting or "role play" than the previous games in the book, though they're still not for "performance." The fun of them is, for the actors, to try on new personalities; and for the observers, to see and recognize familiar and hilarious behavior patterns.

Observing Physical Status:

Status Party

<u>For: Age 9 and up</u>

(From Keith Johnstone)

status; physical; audience

To start "seeing what's happening" with regard to status, I start teaching status by beginning with this game — but I don't tell them what it's for! Sneaky!

How to Play:

Divide the group into two: A's and B's. Tell them that they're all at the same party (feel free to make up a kind of party that they would enjoy). They must walk around and talk to everyone at the party, in the following way: when they're talking to someone, A's should put one hand on the other person's shoulder, and make direct eye contact; B's should touch their own face, and make quick eye contact but then look away. Let them mix and mingle for a couple minutes; then call "Freeze" and have everyone switch to their opposite role and try having a party again.

When the exercise is over, discuss with everyone: what happened?

Coaching Tips:

Let the players make observations first, before chiming in as a facilitator ... but they may well have noticed things like this: The A's probably started talking very loudly, smiling and laughing a lot. The B's probably talked quietly, or maybe with nervous stutters. The A's might have ended up in big groups, while the B's may have ended up together possibly huddled in a corner of the space, or wandering around the periphery. The A's might have been jovially chasing B's around, while the B's stuttered and fled.

Some questions to discuss:

- Which kind of behavior is higher status, A or B?
- Did one kind of behavior feel more comfortable for you?
- Did either kind of behavior remind you of anyone you know?

Watching games like this can be incredibly funny, because it's behavior that people recognize, but it's also here exaggerated to such a degree that it's delightfully ridiculous. To coin a phrase, it's funny 'cause it's true.

Status Tower

For: Age 9 and up

status; physical; audience

Demonstrating physical status through creating a tableau. The fastest way to explore status and stance is to have players try it out, and have everyone else give their feedback. If they've played Status Party first, they probably now have more of a vocabulary to describe what high and low status look like.

How to Play:

Have one volunteer stand in the middle of the space, at neutral: feet parallel and close together, hands at sides, neutral expression. They should remain in that pose throughout the exercise. Ask for another volunteer to come up and stand near the first person; direct them to take a frozen pose that's just a *little* more low-status than the first player. When they've done it, check in with the rest of the group: "Does that look lower status?" If they don't think so, ask for suggestions and modify until they're satisfied. Then, ask for another person to come in and take up a pose that's just a *little* lower status than everyone onstage so far. Again, check in, and modify if necessary. You can keep adding until everyone's in the picture, or until you've determined that you might not be able to get any lower-status.

Bring everyone back, and then talk as a group about what "worked" to achieve a lower-status posture. What did people do with their bodies? Standing? Sitting? Did they move closer to the others, or farther away? Did it matter what their face looked like, or if we could see their face?

Use what happened in that particular tableau to discuss what players actually saw happening.

When you feel ready, now try it with higher status: Start with a first neutral volunteer, and then ask someone to come in and take a pose that's just a *little* higher-status than neutral. Again, check in with the observers and correct if necessary. Continue adding people until it feels like you can't top it, or you run out of players.

Coaching Tips:

The discussion part of this game is especially important, so make sure you check and double check the latest pose before progressing — especially if you as the facilitator see that there might be more to the story. Sure, someone lying in the middle of the floor splayed out might *seem* lower status at first glance; they're sure low to the ground, and don't they look "crazy," isn't "crazy" low-status? ... But look how much attention and space they're taking up. Are they encroaching on other people's personal space? Are they making their own personal space bigger than their own body? Do they seem like they're not protecting their own personal space or body? That seems awfully high-status to me. Conversely, someone crossing their arms angrily might "feel like" they're acting high-status, according to conventional wisdom — but crossing one's arms across one's chest is a protective gesture, and comes off looking lower-status than someone with their hands, say, on their hips.

Let the players come to these conclusions naturally, if you can, but basically physical status is about space and power. A low-status posture is one that protects the person; rather than projecting themselves into the world, they look like they're retreating. This might manifest itself as crossing arms or legs across the body, hunching shoulders to the front, touching one's face, looking away... anything that makes someone look smaller and less present or powerful. High-status positions are ones that project one's personal space outward into the world; you're leaving your soft squishy parts open to the world, because you're confident that no one's going to attack you.

Locating yourself spatially can also convey high or low status: standing behind someone is probably higher status than standing in front of them, because if you're behind them you can see them but they can't see you. Towering over someone is probably a more high-status position than cowering next to them.

The most effective analysis, though, is in actually looking and *seeing* the arrangement of players as they are. Because status and body language make instinctive sense to us, onlookers will often be correct if they just *feel* that a certain pose is high- or low-status.

Observing Verbal Status:

Status Conversations

<u>For: Age 9 and up</u>

status; verbal; partners; group

How to Play:

Every interaction includes a status transaction, and that includes a mere conversation. Speaking to another person carries a status message.

In a two-person conversation, every statement you make is doing one or more of the following:

- Raising your own status
- Lowering your own status
- Raising your partner's status
- Lowering your partner's status

You're going to practice these specific skills, but it's good to investigate them first as a group. Ask the group to come up with examples of each: "What's something you could say to someone else that would raise your own status?" You can bet they'll be able to come up with examples. It would be anything that makes you seem great: "I got an A on that test!" "Like my cool new shirt?" "I'm the line leader today."

Again, let them suggest first, and then check in with the group to see if there's general agreement. Now, when you've asked for examples of each kind of statement separately, see if you can generate combinations:

"What's something I can say that will raise both my status *and* your status?" "What's something I can say that will lower my status and raise yours?" The insidious one: "What's something I can say that will raise my own status and lower yours?" They might have an endless supply of that one ... it's how people are mean to each other while acting like no one notices and no one can do anything about it.

As students are no doubt well aware, status can also include tone of voice, in addition to word content. You can say "Nice shirt!" to someone and raise their status, or say "Nice shirt!" sarcastically and lower their status. The same sentence can be used in all four categories.

This is fun to practice; you could have a volunteer come up and try to say one sentence in all of the four different ways: raising their own status, lowering their own status, raising someone else's status, and lowering someone else's status. Have them try each, and then have the observers comment on whether it worked or not, and why not.

Then, break everyone up into partners, and have them have a series of short conversations, 30 seconds to a minute, where they try out each of the following in turn:

- Each just raise their own status
- Each just lower their own status
- Each just raise their partner's status
- Each just lower their partner's status
- Lower both of their statuses
- Raise both of their statuses
- Raise self and lower other
- Lower self and raise other

You could also designate an A and B in each partnership, and make up combinations such as:

- A raises B, B lowers A
- A raises self; B raises A
- A raises self; B lowers self

You could also have the players suggest combinations — possibly based on people or situations they might have in mind.

Coaching Tips:

After this exercise, have people talk through it. What happened? Was it fun? Were there combinations that were more fun than others? Were there combinations that seemed to fight a lot? Were there combinations that seemed to "work" better than others? Did some of those situations seem familiar? What else did they notice?

Sometimes when we're thinking of raising and lowering status, we're thinking in terms of being mean to each other. That can often be the case, especially when kids, who often have little power of their own, are trying to find ways to gain power over others. These practice conversations might turn toward people being mean. If characters are mean to each other, that's one thing; it's fun and cathartic playing the villain. What we want to avoid is the actual *actors* taking advantage of the opportunity, to take each other down, so be on the lookout for that.

Raising and lowering status also doesn't have to be mean in order to be effective, as might come up in discussion. See if players can think of situations on TV or in real life where there are high-status characters who are not mean (Superman; an awesome principal or teacher), and low-status characters who aren't scared of others or victims of others (Eeyore, Piglet).

Being mean and scary is the obvious way to be high status; challenge your players to have conversations where they practice being high status but super friendly — and the most insidious method is to be high status and ... not necessarily friendly, but *polite*. (This is where Oscar Wilde's best quips come from.)

It's probably going to be challenging for some kids to practice status behaviors that are unfamiliar to them. That's why it's important that they *do* practice them all, and that they practice them in a safe environment. Just like the game of building the tower versus knocking it down, we're urging everyone to consciously try out the full range of behaviors, to prove that they *can* behave in many different ways — and that the behaviors they're personally accustomed to are, like it or not, consciously or not, a *choice.*

Status Card Party

For: Age 9 and up

status; physical; verbal; group

You'll need: A deck of ordinary playing cards, or a stack of numbers written on index cards or slips of paper (at least two sets of numbers 1-10).

How to Play:

When everyone has had a rudimentary runthrough of status, you can play this fun game. Have everyone draw a card, and NOT look at it; they should instead hold it up to their forehead, facing out. Now, tell them that they're at a party where they'll get to see the queen, so they must all be on their best behavior.

At the sign to begin, they should start to interact with everyone at the party. The card on your forehead signifies your status: ace is high; two is low. You can't see your own card, of course, but you can see others', so treat them according to their status (still on your best behavior, of course — be polite!).

Let them go for a while, and then when it seems like they're ready, announce, "It's time to see the queen! Line up right here in order of importance!" Before they look at their own cards, they must give their best guess and line up in order from highest status to lowest; when everyone's found a place in line, they are allowed to look at their cards to see how they did.

I bet they did pretty darn well. Now try it again!

Coaching tips:

If you have a big enough group, it might be worth dividing the players in half for one round and letting them each watch a party, because this game is *fascinating* to watch. And usually hilarious. How quickly people shift their status, even physically, at the first sign that someone's raising or lowering them unexpectedly. You might have people with the same number, either in furious conversation trying to determine their own status, or else staunchly convinced that their own number is much higher than their conversation partner's, when in fact it is the same. Often the high-status people end up in convivial groups at the center of the room, while low-status people skirt the perimeter, looking for someone to talk to. And this all happens as if by magic, the only instruction being cards on foreheads. It is rare that the lineup at the end isn't at least 80% correct on the first try; this is a situation that people seem to viscerally understand.

It's definitely worth playing this game more than once, even before talking about what happened the first time, to give people the chance to play two different statuses (or wind up with the same). (And, because this game is awfully fun.)

I emphasize that players should be on their best behavior and try to be polite to each other during this party, because then they have to find ways to treat lower-status people other than obvious leave-me-alone statements ("Ew, you smell!"). Trying to sound polite also happens to be closer to the way we treat each other in real life, especially as we get older (fourth graders and even eighth graders have been known to issue an "Ew, you smell!" but high schoolers and adults are typically more subtle, especially in public). Just like the first exercises in the book, where we practice knocking down the tower and then building up, we're spurring players to replicate both constructive and non-constructive behavior, so they can really see and feel the difference, both on the giving end and the receiving end.

Secret Status Numbers

<u>For: Age 9 and up</u>

group; audience; status; physical; verbal

This game gives us a common vocabulary shorthand to further define and describe status.

How to Play:

Here are the descriptions of the status numbers. Experience has taught me that a scale of 1-4 works well, and I explain it to everyone like this:

1: The highest status, they feel *most comfortable* when everyone in the room is below them.

2: The second-highest status; they feel *most comfortable* when there's one person higher than them, and everyone else below them. They like having someone to report to.

3: They feel *most comfortable* when there are two people above them and one person below them. They prefer being near the bottom of the ladder, but they like having one person who reports to them.

4: The lowest status: they feel *most comfortable* when they are below everyone in the room.

The "most comfortable" is key; it's the place in the pecking order where they feel like they fit. This tends to make the scenes more emotionally neutral and more interesting, since the characters aren't directly looking for conflict. They're just trying to fall into their preferred status naturally, by maneuvering themselves to that ranking in the room. You might ask if those descriptions remind the players of anyone they know.

Once I've explained the numbers to everyone, I start running through little scenarios, with two people at a time. I give them very, very simple situations with no implied conflict, since we just want to give the characters the barest thread of an excuse to interact. I typically rotate between a job interview, a new-roommate interview or a house meeting, and maybe working on a group project for school. The company or the project doesn't matter really at all; if they're having trouble deciding, you can declare it for them. The important part is what the characters have to say to each other, and even more important than that is HOW they say it.

Step One: For the first two volunteers and their scenario, tell them out loud which status number they'll be playing: they'll each have their own number, 1 through 4. Give them a scenario, and let them talk a little bit. Then, pause the scene and ask the observers how the people onstage are doing: are they accurately portraying their status numbers? If the observers have comments, have the two players adjust, and continue a little bit. After a minute or so, you can end the scene and have some more people try again, maybe with different numbers.

Step Two: After a few rounds with public numbers, play a few rounds where the players secretly choose their own numbers. Again, give them a simple scenario and let them go. After a minute or so, pause the scene and see if the observers can guess what number they each picked. I usually hold my hand over each player's head and say, "Don't tell us your secret number yet, but everyone raise your hand if you think she's being a one? A two? A three? A four?" I'll then say to the players, "If that's different from what you thought, see what you can do to play your own status more." You can go through another couple of rounds like this.

Step Three: This time, you're going to give them each a secret number by whispering in their ear. The point of this round is to play around with expectations: give players a number that you think might be different than what their own default status seems to be. Try giving the loud class clown a four, and the timid shy retreater a one. Another way to play with expectations is to give both players the same number—especially if it hasn't happened on its own yet. Yet again, pause the scenes after a little bit and check with the observers about what statuses they're seeing; have the players adjust if necessary and let the scene play a little farther.

Step Four: You could add another hurdle by adding a third person to the scenes. (I still use the same three basic scenarios.) Again, give them each a secret number. Now that there are three people, it's a lot of fun to add some more opportunities to jockey for status: have three ones, or a one and two two's, so that they're each trying to be second banana. Make them all fours, and watch them try to out-low-status each other. As before, check in with the observers either in the middle, if you see they need some adjusting, or at the end of the scene.

Once everyone's gotten the hang of status, you could even let the observers take turns assigning everyone in a scene a secret number; they might have thought of a combination of numbers that would be fun to see. Or, you can have them draw cards (have several sets of cards labeled one through four), and see what happens when the statuses are truly random.

Coaching Tips:

Especially if there are three people in a scene, remind them as a general rule not to talk over each other. Players should keep an eye on the give and take between them.

On a conceptual level, it might seem confusing to have two (or three) people in a scene, but four possible numbers. The question becomes one of degree and comfort: a scene with a one and a four in it will have a very high-status person, and a very low-status person. In a scene with a two and a three, their statuses will be closer together, and also uneasier: the two is the higher-status character, though they may not be comfortable with that; the two may feel the need to "check in" with the three from time to time, so the two doesn't have to feel like the highest authority in the room.

This game is really fun to watch. The scenario should remain focused on the status relationship; don't let them get too wrapped up in planning and plotting, but urge them to keep trying to maintain their own status number above all else. If they're too concerned with making real plans, have one of them offer the other something to eat, maybe, or a cup of tea. Have them play their status while doing that activity: maybe a low-status person is too shy to take the cup, or else two high-status people fight over which one of them is going to pour the tea. We also don't need to see them actually complete the activity in the scenario; it's fine if we do, but whether the person gets hired or not, or they decide to let the new roommate move in or not, or whether they figure out their school project or not, is unimportant. You can cut the scene when it feels "over" or just when it's been long enough.

Players also benefit from discussing this game. What did they notice about playing high-status numbers versus low-status numbers? Did they play a number that they wouldn't normally play? How did it feel? Did watching it make them think of anything?

Status Switch

For: Age 9 and up

group; audience; status; physical; verbal

An exercise for both sharing control, and observing status relationships that are dynamic instead of static.

How to Play:

Two players are onstage; choose ahead of time which one will start out high status and which low status. Then you can give them a simple scenario: teacher and student discussing homework, two bakers making a cake, etc. Assign each person their role in the scenario — and you don't have to give the traditionally high-status role to the high-status character. In the teacher/student scene, what happens if the teacher starts out low status to the student?

Have the players begin playing their roles, taking care to maintain their own high or low status. The first few times you play it, the facilitator can initiate the change: after about a minute, call "Switch!" at which point the characters should slowly begin to switch their statuses, from high to low or vice-versa. You can choose an arbitrary point in the interaction to call "switch," because the characters can use whatever's going on as an excuse to change their own status. When the scene seems "over," you can call an ending.

Coaching Tips:

Because of, oh, human nature, the high-status player is probably not going to want to switch and let the other person gain higher status than them. You'll likely have to coax them into "losing." This exercise is the role-playing version of Tug-o'-War (page 222): for someone to win, the other person has to lose. Of course, going from high to low status does not automatically mean "losing," but often when playing this game the high status character gives over their control of the situation as they switch to low status. Sometimes the hardest challenge you can issue to young people (and often adults as well) is to play a character who loses in the end.

When role-playing on their own, trying to play "Pretend" or making up their own stories, this moment of switching statuses is a situation that often causes disagreements: when no one will agree to lose at the end of the story, the bad guy and the good guy can get into an *actual* fight, and play devolves into scuffle, or "competition": maybe they start playing a game that can actually be lost or won. Even *then*, the disagreements can continue: the person who ends up losing may have a meltdown, trying to convince the others how they really haven't lost at all because of some technicality. When playing the game of status switching, you can talk with your small charges about this situation: what are the differences and similarities between playing a game, having a fight, and telling a story?

Funny-Cool-Scary

<u>For: Age 9 and up</u>

group; audience; status; physical; verbal

(Modified from Keith Johnstone)

This may be my very favorite game to watch, ever. I find it endlessly fascinating, so I often make my students (and my adult actors) play it. Keith Johnstone plays this game adult-wise with "funny-sexy-smelly," but I've tweaked it so that it's more kid-friendly and gender-neutral.

How to Play:

Four people are in the "scene." Each one should look at the other three characters, and secretly cast these three "roles" in their mind:

- One of the other three is really funny, and you're already pals.
- One of the other three is really really cool, and you hope they'll let you be their friend.
- One of the other three is kind of scary… and you'd rather not hang out with them.

Make sure to emphasize that it's the way your *character* feels about their *character*, not the actor (to head off any hurt feelings). You should not start the scene until each person has secretly identified their fellow players — they should have exactly one of each: a funny person, a cool person, and a scary person. They should individually decide *before* the scene starts, and not change their mind midstream, no matter what happens.

When they've all decided, you can begin: They're all going to a party; pick one of the four onstage to be the party's host. Send the other three offstage, and let the party host start setting up: chairs, snacks, etc. One by one, gradually, the other three people should ring the doorbell and enter the party. We see the host greet each new guest, and we're delighted by their interactions, that hopefully clearly show us what each has decided about the other. Eventually everyone will be there at once, interacting together. You might need to sidecoach, "Get closer to your cool person! Try to stay away from your scary person!"

When everyone's been there interacting for a while, check in with the players: I pause the scene, and then say, "Everyone point to your funny person! Everyone point to your scary person! Everyone point to your cool person!" Now that we can see the relationships, you might give them some further direction to intensify their reactions, just to see what more fun things happen; then you can end the scene and do another round.

Coaching Tips:

The first few rounds, there may be people running all around the stage, trying to get towards and away from each other, which is pretty funny. Once they've had a chance to get the obvious tactics out of their system, probably to great laughter, do a few more rounds with more subtlety. Similar to the Status Card Party, give the direction that everyone at the party should be extremely polite to each other, and try to find sneaky ways of getting closer to someone and farther from someone else, without obviously hurting their feelings.

This game is funny to watch because it even more closely recreates the complex web of relationships that we have with the different people we know. We laugh because it's familiar. Sometimes situations might crop up that hit particularly close to home for players. Someone might end up being the person everyone thinks is cool; someone might end up being the person everyone thinks is scary. You can discuss this with your group; how did this feel to watch? to be a part of? A magical thing that theater can do is show us things that we would never want to happen; part of why this game is so funny and fun to watch is that sometimes people are clearly being awful towards each other, and that's both true and something we don't want to happen to us. By playing out status relationships in this way, we can become more accustomed to recognizing them, moving through them, and if necessary changing them.

NOTES ON STATUS

With great power comes great responsibility, as Spiderman says.

With these games and exercises, we're trying on different statuses, and watching different relationships play out, for a few reasons. One reason is simply to point out the tactics and strategies that people employ in order to portray a certain status. As they may have learned through actually *doing* it, any person can change their physicality and their way of speaking in order to adopt any status. Therefore, any person can also consciously employ those tactics in Real Life. When I teach singing, sometimes younger girls shy away from singing high notes in their head voice "like an opera singer" because it sounds weird to them, and not like "their voice." I tell them in response that any of the sounds they can make, they're allowed to claim as their own voice. Just because it's unfamiliar, it doesn't mean it's not yours. You are allowed to claim all the possibilities in your own mind and body. Similarly, just because you're not used to behaving in a certain way — standing up straight, uncrossing your arms — it doesn't mean that doing those things is "lying" or pretending to be someone else. All of your possibilities belong to you.

Another result of playing through different variations of relationship setups is that players learn to see the mechanics behind these interactions. The closer one begins to pay attention to status relationships in real life, the more obvious they become. That in turn dissolves the mystery around the power wielded by high-status people in real life: "Oh, I see… they're just trying to be high status right now." We start to learn that we can match status with people, in order to better communicate with them — good friends will often mirror each other's status. We start to notice the reasons behind people's behavior, which can give us more useful information about how to navigate situations.

For example, someone you know might walk up to you and say something insulting right to your face. Now, insulting them right back might result in a fight: or else you might deny it, they might say it again, you both might end up yelling at each other — or worse. But having thought about status, you can now see that that person's real aim, even if they don't exactly realize it themselves, is to lower your status and raise their own. You can see more of the existing information in a conversation, which allows you to better communicate and respond.

If your group is interested, you can play with status scenarios that might happen in real life, as a way to see how they might deal with them well (or for fun, how they might deal with them extremely poorly). Everything is a status interaction: baby refusing to eat Mom's broccoli, bully attempting to start a fight, employee asking for a raise, parent giving child an allowance... set them up as scenes, and give them status numbers — and possibly have them switch statuses halfway through the scene. Play them out, see what happens. Discuss the results. Have fun and laugh a lot.

I hope that everyone who starts thinking about status (and improv in general) will use their newfound powers for good instead of evil. It can be an especially powerful tool to help young people understand others, as they navigate the difficult terrain between elementary school and high school. Hopefully learning about thinking constructively, embracing their own ideas, playing well with others, and adapting their behavior to the situation will help them with the ultimate task at hand: to grow into their best selves.

APPENDIX
THE SECOND

Lists of games you can play in specific environments or situations

In the CAR!

Clearly, it's not a place you can move around much, or turn to face one another. But verbal and storytelling games work very well in this setting.

- Alphabet Lists! *(page 128)*
- Word-at-a-time rules, story, or expert *(page 110)*
- Color/Advance *(page 250)*
- Fortunately/Unfortunately *(page 255)*
- That's Better/That's Worse *(page 258)*
- Three Things! *(page 130)*
- Story Spine *(page 244)*
- Counting to 10 *(page 126)*

Games for Moving Around

This is a list of games for players who like to move their bodies — and who happen to be in a physical area, either outdoors or indoors, that's good for moving around.

- Bibbity-bibbity-bop *(page 163)*
- Pass the Clap *(page 172)*
- Clown Circle *(page 175)*
- Boom, Baby *(page 193)*
- Match My Rhythm *(page 196)*
- Fill the Space *(page 179)*
- Mirror *(page 182)*
- Transformation Circle (Copy/Paste) *(page 190)*
- I am a Tree *(page 187)*
- Spacewalk *(page 200)*
- Statues *(page 201)*
- Opposites *(page 205)*
- Find the Thing *(page 209)*
- Imaginary Activity (Extras) *(page 216)*
- Imaginary Sports *(page 219)*
- Tug o' War *(page 222)*
- Dolphin Training *(page 224)*
- Diamond Dance *(page 234)*
- Give and Take *(page 237)*
- Sheep und Wolf *(page 241)*

Games for Outside

These games would be easy to play specifically outside, in an open space.

- Any circle games *(page 133)*
- Any ball games *(page 149)*
- BALL (with a real ball) *(page 150)*
- Pass the Clap *(page 172)*
- I am a Tree *(page 187)*
- Transformation Circle (Copy/Paste) *(page 190)*
- Statues *(page 201)*
- Imaginary Sports *(page 219)*
- Sheep und Wolf *(page 241)*
- Tug o' War *(page 222)*
- Dolphin Training *(page 224)*
- Diamond Dance *(page 234)*
- Give and Take *(page 237)*
- Opposites *(page 205)*
- Spacewalk *(page 200)*

Games for Two

Two can play these games — or a group, divided into partners.

- Color/Advance *(page 250)*
- Fortunately/Unfortunately *(page 255)*

- Word-at-a-Time Story *(page 114)*
- Word-at-a-Time Writing *(page 116)*
- Thing-at-a-Time Drawing *(page 118)*
- Three Things *(page 130)*
- Dolphin Training *(page 224)*
- Story Spine *(page 244)*
- Gibberish Dictionary *(page 153)*

Games for One

You can play these games all by yourself, or you can set them up for someone to play by themselves.

- Color/Advance in writing or art, with a timer *(page 250)*
- Alphabet Lists, either written or spoken *(page 128)*
- Story Spine *(page 244)*

For Quiet Time

These games would be good to play with a group of players (or a class) in a situation where the overall group should be relatively quiet.

- Color/Advance, written in groups or solo *(page 250)*
- Thing-at-a-time Drawing *(page 118)*
- Word-at-a-time Story or Letter, written *(page 116)*
- Line-at-a-time Story or Poem, written *(page 117)*
- Morphing Space Object Circle *(page 198)*

- Yes/Go, the silent version, with nodding *(page 135)*
- Clown Circle, the silent version with gesture only *(page 175)*
- Fill the Space *(page 179)*
- Story Spine, written *(page 244)*
- String of Pearls, written *(page 260)*

For Writing

The games below would be good for writing games and exercises, either working solo or else working in small groups with papers passed between players. You could also try any games that are verbally-focused: even First Letter/Last Letter Ball *(page 157)* or Gibberish Dictionary *(page 153)* might make a good writing game for your specific group or purposes.

- Word-at-a-time Story or Letter *(page 116)*
- Line-at-a-time Story or Poem *(page 117)*
- Story Spine *(page 244)*
- String of Pearls *(page 260)*
- Introduce Your Neighbor *(page 146)*
- Imaginary Environment *(page 212)*
- Color/Advance *(page 250)*
- Fortunately/Unfortunately *(page 255)*
- That's Better/That's Worse *(page 258)*

Making and Exploring Music and Dance

- Note-at-a-time Chord *(page 119)*
- Thing-at-a-time Soundscape *(page 122)*
- Match My Rhythm (bodies, voices, or instruments) *(page 196)*
- Mirror *(page 182)*
- Diamond Dance *(page 234)*
- Give and Take *(page 237)*
- Opposites *(page 205)*
- Story Spine *(page 244)*

Making Art

- Thing-at-a-time Drawing *(page 118)*
- Introduce Your Neighbor *(page 146)*
- Fill the Space *(page 179)*
- Opposites *(page 205)*
- Imaginary Environment *(page 212)*
- What Comes Next? *(page 231)*
- Story Spine *(page 244)*
- Color/Advance *(page 250)*

BIBLIOGRAPHY

Here's a list of books that I've referred to in this book, and which I use often in my teaching. Some of them are the original sources or inspirations for the games contained in *Managed Mischief*. These certainly aren't the only books about improv that are available; they're just the ones I think about the most often. If you're interested in reading more about improvisation or the theater, read some of these!

Bernard, Jill. *Jill Bernard's Small Cute Book of Improv.* N.p.: YESand.com Publishing, 2012.

Brook, Peter. *The Empty Space.* N.p: Penguin Books, 1990.

Barker, Clive. *Theater Games: A New Approach to Drama Training.* London: Methuen Drama, 1989.

Johnstone, Keith. *Impro.* New York, NY: Routledge, 1992.

Johnstone, Keith. *Impro for Storytellers.* London: Faber and Faber Limited, 1999. (Available as an e-book)

Joyce, Mary. *First Steps in Teaching Creative Dance: A Handbook for Teachers of Children, Kindergarten through Sixth Grade.* Palo Alto, CA: Mayfield Publishing Company, 1973.

Koppett, Kat. *Training to Imagine: Practical Improvisational Theatre Techniques to Enhance Creativity, Teamwork, Leadership, and Learning.* Sterling, VA: Stylus, 2001 (Available as an e-book).

Nachmanovitch, Stephen. *Free Play: Improvisation in Life and Art.* New York: Jeremy P. Tarcher/Putnam, 1990. (Available as an e-book)

Rooyackers, Paul. *101 Drama Games for Children: Fun and Learning with Acting and Make-Believe.* Alameda, CA: Hunter House, 1998. (Available as an e-book)

Madson, Patricia Ryan. *Improv Wisdom: Don't Prepare, Just Show Up.* N.p: Bell Tower, 2005. (Available as an e-book)

Spolin, Viola. *Improvisation for the Theater: A Handbook of Teaching and Directing Techniques.* Northwestern University Press, 1999. (Available as an e-book)

Spolin, Viola. *Theater Games for the Classroom: A Teacher's Handbook.* Evanston, IL: Northwestern University Press, 1986.

INDEX OF GAMES

Arranged alphabetically:

Alphabet Lists!	128
BALL!	150
Bibbity-Bibbity-Bop	163
Boom, Baby!	193
Chair Game	228
Character Movements (see Opposites)	205
Circle Pattern Games	137
Circuits (see You)	138
Clown Circle	175
Color/Advance	250
Copy/Paste (see Transformation Circle)	190
Counting to 10 Together	126
Diamond Dance	234
Dolphin Training	224
Extras (see Imaginary Activity)	216
Fill the Space	179
Find the Leader (Rhythm Maker, Mirror in a Circle)	96
Find the Thing	209
First Letter, Last Letter Ball	157
Follow the Follower	99
Fortunately/Unfortunately	255

Funny-Cool-Scary	291
Gibberish Ball	153
Gibberish Dictionary (see Gibberish Ball)	153
Give and Take	237
Go (see Yes)	135
Haunted Museum (see Statues)	201
I am a Tree	187
Imaginary Activity ("Extras")	216
Imaginary Environment	212
Imaginary Sports	219
Introduce your Neighbor	146
Leave the Room for the Same Reason	102
Line-at-a-time Poem	117
Match My Rhythm	196
Mirror	182
Mirror in a Circle (see Find the Leader)	96
Morphing Space Object Circle	198
Museum Guard (see Statues)	201
Note-at-a-Time Chord	119
One-something-at-a-time	109
Opposites (or, Character Movements)	205
Pass the Clap	172
Practice Building the Tower	90
Practice Messing Up!	92
Practicing Knocking down the Tower	87
Red Ball	158
Rhythm maker (see Find the Leader)	96
Secret Status Numbers	285
Sheep und Wolf:	241
Sound Ball	155

Spacewalk	200
Statues (Wax Museum; Museum Guard)	201
Status Card Party	282
Status Conversations	278
Status Party	273
Status Switch	289
Status Tower	275
Story Spine	244
String of Pearls	260
That's Better!/That's Worse!	258
Thing-at-a-time Drawing	118
Thing-at-a-time Soundscape	122
Three Things!	130
Transformation Circle (Copy/Paste)	190
Tug o' War	222
Wax Museum (see Statues)	201
What Comes Next	231
What's Different?	95
Whoosh-Bang-Pow	168
Word Bridges	142
Word-Association Pattern Game (see Word Bridges)	142
Word-at-a-time (Sentences or Rules)	110
Word-at-a-Time Character/Expert	112
Word-at-a-time Story	114
Word-at-a-time Writing	116
Yes (or Go)	135
You (or "Circuits")	138
Zip-Zap-Zop	160

- Focus
- Quiet Time
- Writing
- Art
- Music
- Memory
- Verbal
- Physical
- Rapid-Fire
- Partners
- Circle
- Group
- Audience

 Focus

 Quiet Time

 Writing

 Art

 Music

 Memory

 Verbal

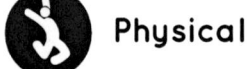 Physical

 Rapid-Fire

 Partners

 Circle

 Group

 Audience

CPSIA information can be obtained
at www.ICGtesting.com
Printed in the USA
LVOW08s1424280217
525679LV00026B/626/P